Making *Youth* Matter

Creating Legacy Through Community

Robert Mitchener

Making Youth Matter

Cover Designed by: perfect_designx

Making Youth Matter book proceeds will be contributing to the development of the Our Youth Matters private charter school foundation fund.

All Interior Photos are from Robert Mitchener's personal collection.

Sponsor testimonials in their entirety can be read on the Our Youth Matters website at www.ouryouthmatters.org

The Community Pages interviews were created through the generous time given to Our Youth Matters from supporting staff, friends, community partners, mentors and dedicated volunteers and board members.

Printed in the United States of America

ISBN: 978-1-66784-446-6

"I could talk about Mitchener all day long, because when I see him – bottom line, I see in him that I have achieved something in the classroom where I was teaching. As an educator that is inspiring to see something you have poured into become an establisher of better and greater things, and that's really the main thing."

Eugene Weeks,
Former Raleigh City Councilman for District C, North Carolina

"The work that Robert Mitchener and the Our Youth Matters team do is critical to helping young people who are at-risk and their success both in school and when they graduate…Keep up the great work!"

Roy Cooper,
Governor, North Carolina

"I am very impressed with Robert for the young man he was in middle school and the man he has grown up to be. He is really doing stuff for students. He is taking the time to give back and develop our young people. It's wonderful and I am proud of him."

Mrs. Doris Frazier,
Retired Educator

"Robert's strongest qualities with youth are being patient and listening to them. He has a way of communicating with youth and building a rapport that gets them to understand better not only what they NEED to do, but what they CAN do."

Clarence "Chucky" Brown Jr.,
Former N.C. State basketball player,
All-ACC first-teamer and NBA Champion

"Robert is color blind, ability blind, blind to all things except that **there is good in everybody**. He is a truthful example of selfless commitment motivated by love for others."

Courtney Crowder,
Managing Director, APCO Worldwide, Raleigh

"No matter what someone is doing or has done, Robert always sees the best in anyone, especially young people. Robert doesn't treat children as though they should have an adult mind when they are only children. Robert sees and models that we have to encourage them where they are to spur the growth of their minds in the most positive way."

Zell Lucas,
President, Lucas Transportation, Inc.

"How many people in law enforcement are still wanting to work with kids after seeing them on the wrong side of things? Robert is making the effort to see that there is another side to the story by digging his heels into the community to find out and make changes from the base place, right where they are and live. How many are doing this? This is why I wanted to become a part of what Robert is doing because I desire to see this grow and develop and help my own community where I live."

Chris Thomas,
Legendary Comedian & Host of The Chris Thomas Show,
Mayor of BET's Rap City

"I am very proud of what Robert has accomplished and prouder of the fact that he is still pushing which is great. He hasn't let Our Youth Matters go and the future is really big for where Robert is taking it next."

Coach John H. Baker III,
Southeast Raleigh High School Educator

"Robert's story speaks about the passion to invest in others. For the young people who might not have somebody at home, or in their group or sphere of friends speaking into their life, Robert's desire is to be that person who can coach and guide them in the right direction. My prayer for Robert is that he continues to receive and walk in a path of even greater success."

Mrs. Darien Young,
Longtime Friend and Raleigh Native

"Robert is a very intentional innovator who has found the most interesting and creative ways to congregate youth within environments that are positive, empowering and safe. That is a need in our community now. We need more of that, and I am glad that someone with his dogged determination is at the helm of an organization like Our Youth Matters."

Alfredo Hicks,
Childhood Friend, Raleigh, NC

"Robert has a way of surprising people with what he does. It's not like he has a large platform or a stage or a spotlight like pro's or celebrities but he goes hard and produces the most excellent things within his power as though he did have them. I admire him for that, and even with writing his story it all goes back to what really makes him tick-- helping every young person that he can."

Kerwyn Hinton,
Childhood friend, Raleigh, NC

"We have a common love of serving our community of youth. Making sure they get the love and support that they need. We often bounce ideas off of one another of how to be a better support to those in our community and what initiatives we both can drive home to be supportive of each other in our endeavors."

Tomiko Hicks,
Wake County, HS-ESS Assistant Division Director - Child Support Services

"A lot of people come from situations that are bad but they can turn their lives into something good. However, in order for that to happen we need people like Robert Mitchener who reach out into the community and remind our youth they have value. I'm so very proud of you brother!"

Michael Colyar,
Actor, Comedian, Author, Host of The Michael Colyar Show

DEDICATION

I dedicate this book to Mr. Lem Barney. You saw a young man working at the Sheraton Imperial Hotel who you did not know at all and you invited me into your life.

Thank you God for Lem Barney, who entered my life as a true angel. Angels are messengers who bring you good news. Mr. Lem Barney, I want you to know that is exactly what you poured into my life—Good News. I have chosen to continue to spread that same news to every life I touch.

You are a constant inspiration to every part of my life and soul. Thank you for everything you freely gave to a young kid from Southeast Raleigh.

I will forever remember and keep your words of wisdom:

"Robert, always remember, 'Yes I Can' = the meaning: Yes, you can do anything and everything you put your God-given mind to. Jesus is Lord & Love and I love you also." **—Lem Barney**

CONTENTS

FOREWORD

Communities are filled with potential world changers, it's up to those who have abilities, resources and influence to dig out, dust off and develop those future leaders among our youth so they shine like the diamonds they were born to be.

Robert and I met back in the early 90's or 2000's. Hard to believe that's been almost a lifetime ago. We met through my dad John H. Baker, Jr. who was a professional NFL football player, Sheriff and former Chairman of Wake County. His teammate and friend Lem Barney had come into town for a function. Robert encountered Lem Barney at his Hotel during that time which began their friendship. Later on, Lem introduced Robert to my Dad who at the time of their meeting was the Wake County Sheriff. This grew a relationship between Robert and him eventually leading Robert into the arena of law enforcement.

We got more acquainted with one another through basketball. He played at Broughton High School before me but I had heard about him from friends that knew him. I was a schoolteacher then and had begun running a basketball camp that ran for a number of years. I invited Robert to be a counselor at my basketball camp and that cemented our connection. It has been a lifelong relationship since then. In those early days of working alongside me at my basketball camp, Robert worked late shift. He would get off work from patrol and come in after not sleeping and work a full day of basketball camp every day—week after week. I commended him, because I thought it was marvelous that he dedicated himself to those kids so wholeheartedly as an unpaid volunteer. Since he had been a former basketball player and was working in law enforcement, it was a match made in heaven. He knew what he was talking about basketball wise and then was also very familiar with what was going on in the community as a Deputy Sheriff. The kids always took to him as far as him being a counselor and they learned a great deal from him not only about basketball but even more about life. I am now a retired Coach and Teacher but even in my retirement, I am still a very involved hands on partner of the molding and building of relationships with our communities youth.

Much of that interaction is predominantly through working, partnering and collaborating with Robert on numerous events and activities with his Our Youth Matters project.

When he first approached me to collaborate, I was a High School basketball coach and High School PE teacher in Southeast Raleigh. He would always run ideas past me and we would tweak them and see which way we could go at it, and he involved a whole lot of kids who attended Southeast Raleigh. Many of them were very instrumental and benefitted greatly from their experiences with Our Youth Matters. Robert also paid close attention to incorporating their feedback as well.

Many youth who were a part of Our Youth Matters then are now involved in their community doing great things and taking part in other productive endeavors due to what they were exposed to and learned through the Our Youth Matters events.

There are not enough of this type of organization. Robert's is just one of a few and it should be more.

It's needed for others to just try and take the initiative to just do it because some people are not willing to just go out there and try. They think it may fail but in order for it to work *you have to try*. The key is to start out small and then let it grow and work its way up. Like anything, even when my basketball camp started out with just a couple kids, then grew to a 100 or more a week. It's taking a chance to go out there and do it. Once you start you will get bigger as your ideas grow. Starting a project can become a great legacy to the youth, who in turn take the legacy taught to them to teach others and pass it on. You hear much about this concept, but you don't see enough of it *happening* out there. School teachers can't go over everything that needs to be taught and go over it repeatedly like other organizations who can be involved with youth can do.

We need organizations like Our Youth Matters that can take their influence and apply it in consistent relational layers in the lives of today's youth.

The more people who can jump on board and give their support to organizations like this the better off our youth will be. Hopefully, we can add to it through efforts like this book and the host of events and projects I know Robert has in mind. It would be ideal to have more organizations that really care about the youth and the direction they are going in. Many of my generation were taught by our elders that the youth are the future and what we instill into and teach them is a reflection of what's going to happen with our own future. Robert believes that and is passionate in showing them the right intentions and direction to go in to achieve a better way.

I am like a brother to Robert. We are always in sync, side by side in every endeavor. When he presents a new idea, concept or event, he doesn't have to worry about asking me if I am in or not. I always know it will be something great. I am grateful and honored to always be alongside of what he is doing. I feel almost like I am the elder statesman in our relationship, though I am not that much older than him. But I am very proud of what he has accomplished and prouder of the fact that he is still going. No matter how hard it has gotten; he is still pushing. He hasn't let Our Youth Matters go and the future is really big for where it's going. I think the legacy of him being tutored by my dad and me being tutored by my dad and other great people in the Southeast Raleigh community has been passed on. That is a legacy. My Dad was someone who understood and lived the life of someone who knew celebrity status, working status and even political status. But those items weren't his endgame. He was tireless in always utilizing the resources he came in contact with to find a way to lift others—especially youth. His passion for developing youth and the community was passed on to me and it was passed on to Robert.

And now Robert is striving and reaching forward to continue passing that legacy on with all the knowledge he has gained through his experiences to every youth and life he touches. Being caring, passionate and driven to empower others is a precious legacy to give future generations. I am glad to see this book joining the ranks of Robert's many faceted passions pouring into the lives of our communities and its youth.

John H. Baker III,
Southeast Raleigh High School Educator

ACKNOWLEDGMENTS

I AM GRATEFUL for my parents who through their examples instilled within me the appreciation for hard work, striving for your dreams and always reaching for more.

It is my desire to pass on that very same drive to my daughters who are a part of the future generation I am endeavoring to empower.

Special thanks to everyone who provided their time, treasure, talent and input in so many ways to help make this project happen. I need another book to fill up and name all of you.

And finally, to all of the young people past, present and future who have been a part of building the legacy of Our Youth Matters.

INTRODUCTION

*"Every young person deserves a chance to fulfill their dreams;
because when dreams are realized legacies are born."*

IT IS MY DESIRE that this book inspire young people of all ages, their parents and caretakers to consider the circumstances and situations around you as cues that your life has a purpose. It is not over or in despair or at a dead end or hopeless. You have every chance to turn your impossibilities into possibilities. You can use those moments; pressures, and frustrations as tools to help you choose a better path than you are on today.

As you read some of the things I have seen and experienced may you come to understand that sometimes opportunities come in disguise. And if you can embrace that way of thinking you will soon find yourself discovering a life full of dreams and destiny.

Everything significant in life comes by taking part in small things one step at a time. It's those consistent steps that eventually build up and create your destiny and community for others.

IT TAKES
A COMMUNITY

Lindsay A. Mitchener, *Firstborn daughter of Robert Mitchener Founder of Our Youth Matters. The following is an excerpt from her College Entrance Statement about Community Builders.*

One person in my life that I see as a community builder is my dad. My dad is a Deputy Sheriff Officer. He has provided more than 20 years of service within his community.

My dad has helped to promote community mentoring within Wake County.

And I see my dad as a community builder because he is always wanting to make people happy. Every morning, my dad sends me and my sister videos of him in the morning just doing his normal morning routine, either running on the treadmill or driving to work.

Whenever, my dad sends me a video he is always so happy and lively. My dad often says in the videos (my nickname is sweetcake) "SWEETCAKE GET UP AND BE JOLLY!"

This is very important to me because it gives me an extra boost and pushes me to be better. My dad is always one to want happiness for others rather than himself.

My dad created an organization called Our Youth Matters. Our Youth Matters is a non-profit organization which helps kids who struggle to be better.

When my dad created this organization, he was also going through a tough time himself. During that time he was dealing with a divorce. Through the time, my dad stayed strong and committed to doing what he needed to do to be successful. My dad has always been one to put others before himself.

CHAPTER ONE

BASKETBALL

"Sports do not build character. They reveal it."
Heywood Hale Broun

I just knew that basketball was going to be my life. I ate, slept, played and prayed it every night. It seemed most times to everyone who knew me that basketball was all there was to life and nothing was going to stand in my way to make it all the way to the NBA.

Have you ever prayed, wished and hoped to become something? And as you look at yourself right now; are you in that place you prayed and hoped and wished for?

I grew up in Southeast Raleigh, North Carolina. It wasn't the best where I lived, there was a lot of crime, but it was a good enough, fairly decent neighborhood. Back then I had my sights set on the sport of basketball. I took an interest in it when I went to my oldest first cousins high school basketball game. I was hooked once I saw him take the ball and score doing a slam dunk at the end into the basket. And seeing how the crowd and young kids would all come up shaking his hand, wanting his autograph. Yep, that's when I kind of got bit by the bug of basketball; when I first saw that. It wasn't long after that I started playing a lot of basketball myself. Pickup games, little league and just getting involved with basketball as much as I could. I would play in the neighborhood, during my free time at the park near my house. There was always some type of sports you could play in our neighborhood. As I look back, I realize I played so much basketball. And when I wasn't playing the game, I was praying about it. Many times I would send up my prayers at night before I would go to bed asking God to help me become an outstanding player and to help me go all the way to the NBA. And when I wasn't playing basketball, I spent my time watching and observing people who played. Especially the NBA players on TV. Many of the players I watched had good messages. My idol in those days was Julius Erving, also known as 'Dr. J.' He did a lot of commercials talking about the benefits of having focus and staying off drugs and staying in school. For a kid in my neighborhood, those messages meant a lot for me to aspire to, since every day an opportunity for a life of drugs was always right up in your face in my neighborhood. Sometimes just outside my window. So it could have been easy for me to get into. But that basketball bug had bitten me hard. And to play the dream games I would often see in my daydreams; I just knew I had to stay on the right track.

Having a mother and father who didn't play no games about getting into trouble and having an education didn't hurt either. I was one of the lucky kids who had both parents at home. The laws of the house were: you could play outside but you did your work and your chores around the house and you also went to church. There was no compromising any of those. Especially church. My mom made you go to church every Sunday, and you were not just an attender you were a participator too.

Basketball worked all those angles; it was work, it was fun, you had to faithfully show up and you had to participate. I think that's why my parents let me taking to basketball the way I did and praying everyday so hard to be successful in it created a good foundation in me. Having that as my focus I know is what kept me many a time from heading in directions that might not have played out the best scenarios for me.

That's why I say that God gives everybody a mission or goal, something that He wants you to do in life. And it may not be the road that you want to take. He may take you down a certain or uncertain road to get to another.

This turn of certain versus uncertain is what happened to me. Like I said, I would pray all the time to become an NBA basketball player. And I didn't just pray-I played. Middle school, junior league, and high school. If there was a game at the park or the community center then you would have found me there. And I considered myself to be pretty good. Then as I progressed through my high school years and didn't get a scholarship or even scouted; my thoughts about where my plan was leading even well after I left those high school halls, took a hard look at things. I noticed that, my prayers started working. Only they didn't work for me. Instead, I had a cousin, who seemed to start living the very dream I had been praying so hard for. Every prayer I would pray for myself about becoming outstanding in basketball seemed to jump over me and go straight to him! He actually became quite a star; got a full scholarship into an NCAA Division I team and scouted to be placed on track for the NBA. But something happened. Some bad things took place where he actually lost the scholarship and everything.

However, this didn't deter my own desire and love for basketball. I didn't get to the NBA but the game continued to keep me out of trouble. Some people are in it for the game, the crowds, the fame, etc. Many think those things will bring what they desire. I began to understand that my love for the game brought with it a team of friends. Friends that added strength to my hopes and dreams of doing more in this life. The drive, the prayers, the connections were all collaborating together to play me into the next seasons of my life. Some of those friends that I met playing the game of basketball and praying to be successful at it became key players who helped me later on in my journey to build my youth program and organization. Many of them continue to work with me and the youth of the community to this day. And all because I prayed and played-no matter what the game of life decided to bring.

IT TAKES A COMMUNITY

Darian Young, *Childhood Friend*

We lived in the same neighborhood. Me my mother and brother we lived in the apartments. Right across the street was a housing development; Robert and his family lived in those homes. We went to the same high school, had classes together and that's how we met. I know him as a person. I moved to Charlotte years ago and when I go to Raleigh, I mostly go to see family and I've gotten with him a few times before I head back to Charlotte. I've always kept in contact with him over the years, and it's hard to believe we've known each other now for over 30 years.

The first I can say about Robert is his sense of humor. He has a great sense of humor and he has a way of finding humor in things that maybe you didn't think about. And it never fails every time we talk, we always find something funny to laugh about. I love to laugh so It's a good mix of what both of us bring to the table. Together we can find humor in just about anything.

Another fine quality about Robert is that he cares. He has always been that type of person. He's a leader definitely. He was like that in school. He played sports in school and he definitely was not shy even though he often was someone who liked being put towards the back, since he was never about being seen or whatever. But he's definitely not somebody you are going to run over. He does well at speaking up for himself. He has character and integrity. His mother played a HUGE part in his life and her opinion and her contributions to his life mean so much to him.

When she passed that was a turning point for him. Unlike some, he became even more caring and began to say: 'Ok, how can I give back? What can I do?' His mother was a member of an organization called the Eastern Stars and in that organization those women do community projects and they are very focused on giving back. Robert saw that in her and made the decision to emulate what she did.

His life story, what he has gone through, his experiences, it all feeds into who he is good, bad and the ugly. I think he has turned it around to work for him and out of it has come some great things like his youth organization. Robert has lived the story of what he has created with Our Youth Matters. He is an enactment of what he desires to share with these youth. How a life can take a good turn because of people investing in others who wouldn't otherwise have a starting point for their lives.

> *Robert's story speaks about the passion to invest in others. He took the things that were poured into him and he decided to expand them, broadening the path for others. For the young people who might not have somebody at home, or in their group or sphere of friends speaking into their life, Robert's desire is to be that person who can coach and guide them in the right direction.*

He has pledged that he's going to help these young people by mentoring them into new directions. He has built a really good name in the area and he is now gaining a lot of support from leadership in Raleigh which is definitely encouraging.

Everybody sees success differently and everybody experiences it differently. My prayer for him is that he continues to receive and walk in a path of success that is pleasing and satisfying to him.

CHAPTER TWO

GO AHEAD SON, TELL THEM THE TRUTH

"A Father is someone you look up to no matter how tall you grow."
Unknown

I have 3 sisters, two older and one younger than me. I missed not having a big brother around to cover for me or understand where I was coming from. Southeast Raleigh wasn't the best but it wasn't the worst either. I was good friends with one of my neighbors up until we both got into high school but for the most part people kept to themselves and most times folks were just trying to keep their families safe. Many kids on our street didn't have a lot; but we had fun around the neighborhood the best way we knew how without getting into trouble.

Though my family wasn't well off we all were taught to work hard. When we came of age my Dad had all of us experience helping out with a bill or two from time to time. My first part-time job was at a local drugstore. I also made extra money by cutting grass and making myself useful doing chores around the house.

My mother was strict but loving. She worked at Memorex/Telex a computer plant that made printed circuit boards. My mother always encouraged me to do my best and always celebrated whatever I attempted or achieved. In fact, some of my fondest childhood memories are when I sang in the youth gospel choir and during my elementary years performing in my school's Christmas play. She was also passionate about helping our community as a devoted Eastern Star.

My Dad worked full-time as a correctional officer at Central prison and a second job at a local grocery store. He was a real tough guy, a no nonsense kind of person. My parents didn't always get along very well, because of how rough my Dad would sometimes act but my mother was always good at keeping peace. My father and myself had a decent relationship, but he worked all the time. Even when he was off; he was either working on cars or handyman projects around the house.

He instilled in me the tool of never giving up, to always strive for something higher, and reach for the stars. One thing he would always tell me, "Always dress for success" even if you don't have any money in your pocket, because doing so may get you an opportunity.

He often told me to work hard to get where I wanted to go, because you could have whatever you wanted as long as you worked hard for it.

However, I don't recall *him* ever being much of a dreamer. He was always talking about buying a boat; but he never did. Thinking on that from time to time has made me more committed to accomplishing things I really want to in my life. I've noticed through the years that many people who are in similar situations may not get things because they worry about the cost and often settle for things they don't really want. I've taken this to heart and mixed it with the useful and foundational things my father taught me. Yes, we all should work hard, my father was a stern, hard- working and demanding person. He was hardly ever home, and when he was home, he was in bed. He often just went from one job to the next. I've learned from that way of life.

It taught me the value of a good work ethic. This has been instrumental in assuring my own financial future. But I have also learned the value of spending time with my kids. I spend more time with my girls than my Dad ever spent with me. But when he did spend that time with me it was always a teaching moment. He would say nothing comes for free, you have to work hard for it. This helped me not to entertain what I saw going on in the neighborhood or at the park when people were doing or selling things they weren't supposed to. And I came to understand that having the type of parents I did kept me from desiring those other things. But something I have added to my father's teaching is to not forget that in working hard it's okay to experience the benefits of that hard work, and to remember that there is life going on around you and sharing it with others in your home and community is also a commendable part of your life's work.

Another important lesson my Dad taught me was to be unafraid to take the courageous path of telling the truth while being responsible and respectful in saying so.

When I was young, I was driving home one evening not too far from my house. An officer pulled me over, yanked me out of the car, held me at gun point, spread my body over the hood of the police car and frisked me. My sports car had my nickname "BOOCHIES" on the license plate. The officer said someone with that name had just been shot and killed and that's why they pulled me over and they wanted to take me in for questioning. I asked the officer if I could please let my parents know what was going on. They followed me as I drove to my house. My Dad got so upset. He really let those officers have it! - You got the wrong kid! He kept saying, he does not do any wrong. But then, after my Dad had said his peace to the officers, he turned to me and told me: "Go on down there son, answer all the questions that they want you to answer." Then he turned back to the officers and told them; "Ya'll are wrong. You have the wrong kid because he does not do any wrong." And then my Dad shocked those officers because he went on back to bed. You see my Dad could have said, no son you're not going nowhere with them because I know you ain't done nothing wrong! It could have been a big mess, but instead my Dad said - Go, son; go down there with them go ahead and let them ask their questions and you answer them.

Nowadays, kids are not being directed to do that. I realize many of us look at our current times and think things have gotten out of hand. But, often in my youth program I am teaching youth that choosing to be respectful, intelligent, and integrity focused even in the face of being mistakenly wronged as in my own situation is much more powerful, memorable and in the end admirable. Many scenarios can be handled quickly and easily. But when anyone gives an officer a hard time, it escalates to something else.

When I work with juvenile youth, a common question I ask is: Did you know that officers are trained to think that when you don't provide simple information you have something to hide?

Just having that knowledge empowers youth to calmly consider things before giving officer's a hard time. I have lived what I am expressing here, and I share this story often with youth. My Dad was upset with what happened to me, and I was scared and upset as well. But I will never forget the lesson of re-focusing myself and being courageous enough to be truthful and respectful even in the midst of adversity.

After 30 years at the Central Prison my Dad retired. He had always like cars, and decided to try his hand at having his own Taxi Cab service. He bought three or four of them and drove one himself and rented out the others. By this time, my mother had passed and none of us saw him very much. but I had tried to stay in contact as much as I could. He had been doing pretty well for himself, until one night he picked up a rider and when they got out, they shot up the taxi with him still inside over 9 times. Thankfully, no bullets hit my dad directly, one just grazed his foot. His friend who had also been in the car called me and I asked if he needed me. He said, "No, I know you got to go to work," to which I replied; "I am on my way." I called my sisters to make them aware and they agreed I should go and check it out. When I arrived at the scene the investigator was questioning my Dad and I heard him ask if he was alright. It was at that moment my Dad saw me and told him; I am okay now because my son is here. My Dad had never really been an affectionate person, but he hugged me so tight and cried. That was the first time I had ever seen my Dad cry. Though my sisters were relieved he was ok, they hadn't come with me because they each were still dealing with how things had gone during our childhood years when my Dad hadn't been so good to our mother. Though I remembered many of those times, I had chosen to not hold resentment like that. My mother had never treated my Dad that way and I followed her example of operating in compassion and love instead as well.

Many youth today don't always have the best of circumstances or situations in their homes or lives. But even memories can give us a legacy if we allow them to teach us. This principle has become a special key that I use when mentoring the countless youth I have worked with and continue to work with.

And though both of my parents have since passed well over 20 years ago now; I can still look back with gratitude for what they shared with me and for what they taught me directly and indirectly with their work ethic, determination and love.

IT TAKES
A COMMUNITY

Kerwyn Hinton, *Childhood friend, Raleigh, NC*

My nickname for Robert is Boochie. We were childhood friends and that's what we called him growing up. I can recall a time when we were playing little league baseball together and on our way to the baseball game, we saw a plum tree. I told him to look out for me and I was going to be the one to go out by the tree, and get some plums, but we didn't know that the guy was home, so he came out the house and we took off running, running with all the plums we could actually carry and then we went on to the game.

Then another time there was a plum tree in the neighborhood and we was on our way to play basketball with some of the other kids, we got into this plum tree and I told Boochie to look out for me because I was always the guy who went up the tree and Boochie was always the one on the ground looking out and seeing if anyone was at home. By the time the guy came out of his house again, I came down with broken limbs with plums on them and we both took off running with plums, broken limbs and all. That's about as dangerous as it got for us back then. Another time we rode our bikes all the way from where we lived to North and Crabtree. People thought we were crazy, but we were just kids, maybe about 12 or 13. That was what we did in the summertime, play ball, ride bikes, go to the store and play Ms. Pac-Man. Boochie didn't like Ms. Pac-Man because I would stay all day. I chuckle when I think back on those times we had.

We were both raised with a mom and a dad in the home. A lot of our friends didn't have that. I think that is one of the reasons why we both kept on the straight and narrow. We would be disciplined by our parents and that definitely kept us out of a lot of trouble. We lived right across the street from each other and we would have family cook outs. In the summertime my dad would cook out and we would have what they call *pig pickins*, and my dad would have a pig and his family would come and eat with us. Thinking about that makes me think of all the many good times we have had together.

We played little league, football, basketball, middle school basketball and football together, then

when we got to high school he stuck with basketball and I stuck with football.

After our school days, Boochie joined the Deputy Sheriff Office about 4-5 years before I did
because I went into the military. When I got out
of the military he was already working. I was like
wow you are a deputy now, ok, let me try that. And
through it all we have always remained friends.

I know he cares a lot about youth. There were so
many things we saw coming up and some of our
friends we lost along the way. It was unfortunate
but I know that his whole heart is in the right place
because he doesn't want the kids he works with
now to go through what we had to go through. He
has a big heart and he is a giving person, That's the
thing about Boochie he always puts others before
himself.

When he came to me and told me about Our
Youth Matters, at times it would seem like he was
kind of down. It's not easy starting something on
your own and there are days when challenges come
to test your drive. But I would always tell him remember be encouraged because God gave you this
vision. He could have given it to anybody else but
He gave this vision to **you** for a reason. God looks
at everything we have been through and I really

believe that God is not worried so much about our ability as He is concerned with our **availability**.

When you look at things and you look back in retrospect on how kids like us who come from Southeast Raleigh, with so much going on all around us. Like friends dropping out of school, doing drugs, friends dying young. We both have often wondered: How did all that miss us? It helped that we both had two parents in the home. Parents that cared about us and were motivated about our education and everything else. They cared enough to see that Robert went to college and I went to the military,

And even then as he is now; Robert always would reach for more. He always wanted more.

Robert was always looking for a way to help somebody, He was always looking at a way to get out and bring the community together, to bring kids together, to give someone who didn't have a chance to give them a chance.

Robert has a way of surprising people with what he does. It's not like he has a large platform or a stage or a spotlight like pro's or celebrities but he goes hard and produces the most excellent things within his power as though he did have them. I admire him for that, and even with writing his story it all goes back to what really makes him tick--helping every young person that he can.

A few years ago he actually brought our community together where he gave the local college an award. This was good, but then he also decided to give the High School an award. But you know what the biggest thing was? He had a big table set up for people to *register to vote*. Many of the people who attended that awards event weren't registered to vote and he provided an outlet for them to register. It's those things that we need to see on the TV that don't get talked about but need to be.

Not about this player or that team owner or power broker; whoever is the name of the hour in the media. I couldn't even imagine if Boochie had half of that, what he would do. Seriously, that is what we look at. Many say they are going to give so many millions to this or that and we are going to do a backpack drive and that's all good. But how about just donating outright to the school? How about buying all those things (backpacks, books, pencils, pens, crayons, etc.) and letting the school distribute those to the people that need it. There are really needy people out here. And let me remind you that the place where we grew up in wasn't the best area. I told him. 'man do you realize that you got all these people together, you found a way to bring all these people out.' The Sheriff's office was there the Police office was there along with all the helpers he got to assist him with registering people to vote. And I remember saying to Robert, 'look at it nobody's fighting and nobody got stabbed, cut, or shot or sold drugs or anything like that.' He even got many of our communities elderly people to come out. That is how powerful his passion is. This is a man who like I have said; doesn't have the platform like other popular media influencers may have or anything in the same league as they do, but I put Robert right up there with them.

Robert has taken on and produced amazing re-sults by utilizing one of the most major key ele-ments our youth in today's society need most. To just sit down, talk and have a conversation. To take the time to *lean in* and listen about what is going on in their world. The things our kids are coming up against today, we didn't have to face. All we knew was playing basketball, football, baseball or going outside to play all day, We didn't have to worry about the stuff going on today like youth do now.

But what they do need today is—Communication. I don't care if you take a kid from the west or east coast; if you start by being *willing* to sit down, you might realize that you actually have more in common than you ever thought possible. All from just sitting and talking. I just don't see enough of people who say they want to come back really come back and get involved with what is going on with the youth from their block or former communities. It starts with being thankful. Be thankful that you can eat out of a clean dish, be thankful that you can sleep on clean sheets at night. Being thankful that you have a roof over your head and clothes on your back. Being thankful that you are not bouncing from house to house wishing there were someone to show you love or to care about you. If today's youth were getting these things at home, they wouldn't be getting into gangs, they wouldn't be out here on the streets doing drugs.

Take the time to tell youth you know and youth who are around you that you care about them. I myself have been inspired at how Robert does this. Now, every chance I get, whenever I am in uniform, I just stop by and see what's going on. I do it with my own kids sitting down with them and talking with them as well. Sure we all have busy lives and jobs and sometimes those

things try to get in the way, but we all should just try to sit down and talk with them and just show them and tell them things. And then—LISTEN to them. Listen about what they got going on.

You can reach back and help out. We all can. Whatever position you are in. If you have a business or you run your own business, and you find out that someone needs help; offer them a job or some time to just be around you. What if by seeing you actively doing your entrepreneur thing, they might begin to think, 'Hey I could do this too. I could have my own business.' That could be empowering to a young person. WE, and I mean ALL of us, don't take enough time to look at what someone else is going through because we look at and get caught up in: I have a roof and clothes, food and money. But what about the ones that don't have it like yourself? Right in this job here I take myself out of my uniform and I put myself in their shoes, even though I am a law enforcement officer. Every person I stop doesn't need a ticket, maybe they just need me to talk to them. Maybe they didn't know their tags were expired. Maybe they lost their job or are going through financial difficulties right now. Maybe they didn't know they were speeding. Maybe we can just give them a word and say, 'hey just try to leave earlier for work or whatever.' Or when I respond to a call at their house, they don't necessarily need to go to jail, maybe they just need someone to talk to.

Over the course of the last 25 years in this job you wear a lot of hats, sometimes people and youth just want to talk and that's it and you are in a position to listen to them, to just let them talk.

What Robert is doing with this is wonderful, I can see it catching on all over the world, because no matter where you would demonstrate it, the principle holds true— Our Youth Matters. It says it all. It means that someone like me who says to the new officers coming on, I am in the back end of my career, 25 years now on this job. You know now is the time to become a change maker and mold them, to plant a seed with them. That is what all of us can and should be doing with any youth we have the opportunity to be around. plant a seed, just give them a word: 'hey son I am glad that your grades are good come on and keep striving because you can be anything you want to be, anything at all. Don't cut yourself short, it may take a bit but you are just laying a foundation.' That's something I always say to my kids, like my son who is in the 7th

grade. I say, "Son right now you are laying a foundation. When you are in elementary school you are just kind of going through but when you hit 5th grade you are like a big fish in the little pond. So, when you go to middle school 6th, 7th and 8th, you are moving up to being a bigger fish in a bigger pond."

Every day we should encourage our youth, I think the more we pour into them the better off we will be.

That's why I always tell Boochie, tell God you are grateful for the vision that He gave you, he could have given this vision to anyone else but He chose you. HE chose you because He knows how you came up. He sees your heart and He knows that you are someone who when He gives you a little something, you are going to stretch it to become bigger and better things.

Robert is always putting others first, and it's never about himself but always about somebody else.

He has sacrificed so much just to give. To make sure a kid could go to camp, even when he brought all the people out to register to vote, he brought in a bass pro fisher. Do you know how big that is someone like that coming into our community? for a kid - who is saying 'man, this guy cares about me?' This guy could be going somewhere else but he cares enough about me to drop in and see what's going on with me? And to teach me something? Wow! Wow! His heart is as big as all the outdoors. It's for moments like that which I have witnessed him doing for youth that keeps me telling him: 'Man keep doing what you are doing, **keep doing what you are doing**.' Robert is a loyal brother that is just awesome and I am so very proud of him.

Our Youth Matters is going to experience an even greater launching, I can already see it. He has taken the time to lay his foundation and it's solid. And he knows that anytime and anything that is needed, I will be right there to join in—always.

CHAPTER THREE

ANOTHER PATH

"Watch and profit by every circumstance."
Henri de Jomini

Sometimes our lives press and position us to be right where we are supposed to be even when we may find ourselves somewhere parallel, opposite or just a completely different place than what we had thought of for ourselves.

In May of 1991, I was working at the Sheraton Imperial Hotel in Raleigh, North Carolina. I remember the Duke Children's Classic Tennis Fundraiser was happening, but for me and my friend it was just another busy weekend getting ready for a big banquet at the hotel. I could never have guessed what was about to happen to me and all because of a table. My friend and I were setting up in one of the grand halls. We were attempting to lift a huge table when suddenly a gentleman called out to us, "Hey Coach, if you don't watch how you are lifting that you might hurt yourself." He then put down the luggage he was carrying and came over to us and proceeded to show us a better way to lift it together. He actually helped us. As we finished up, he introduced himself as Lem Barney, gave us his room number and told us to come upstairs to his room after we got off work so he could talk to us. We both were pretty shocked but once we clocked out, we did just that. When we got to his room; he showed us all the gifts given to him just because he came to participate in the Classic that weekend. He said, "I've been given all of this because I am a celebrity, but I want you to know that I am no different than you, and you can have this too." He then asked us to spend the weekend with him at the Classic. We came back the next day to the Hotel and Lem Barney took us everywhere he went. We watched him play tennis for the Classic. Lem had us ride along with him to all the events he attended. After the events he took us to dinner to hang out with his celebrity friends like Franco Harris of the Pittsburgh Steelers who had come for the Classic as well. Lem Barney treated us like we had been his friends our whole lives. After the weekend was over; I gave Lem my phone number. My friend thought I was crazy because Lem didn't give me his number. I didn't care, I knew how I felt. I had just met and spent time with a legend who treated me like I was one too. It was one of the happiest moments in my life.

I was sleeping in Monday morning, trying to catch some extra sleep before my next shift at the Hotel. My Dad woke me up, "Boochie! Telephone!" When I got over to the phone and asked who it was; Lem Barney said on the other end, "Coach! I forgot to give you my number." I was so excited Lem called me. I told him I wished I could come and see him. The next thing I knew, Lem was saying "Coach you can come see me anytime you want, just get yourself ready and come." He gave me his address and that was that. Lem Barney NFL Legend had just called my house and told me I could come see him whenever I wanted! I floated to work that day and couldn't wait to tell my friend. My friend and I set a date then booked a bus ticket all the way to Springfield, Michigan from Raleigh, North Carolina. That bus ride was LONG! It took us a whole 24 hours to get there. To this day, I have never ridden the bus again. But it was worth it when I arrived. It was a once in a lifetime experience that was about to change my whole life.

I stayed with Lem Barney over three weeks. I was at a time in my life where I had already graduated High School and even tried some College. I had attended Allen University in South Carolina where I studied Business Administration for less than 2 years. I learned from the short time I spent in college the importance of being independent and though I did not remain there; my parents were very supportive of me and my decision. At the time, college didn't seem to have the best fit for me. I only had the plan of taking myself as far as I could go in basketball. And in my mind then, college could not help me with that. So, I was still in my basketball dream fog until I intersected with Lem Barney. Sure, I was working a job but I had no real concrete plans except to be famous one day for my skills like any other young man hooked on the game. I was ripe for another path. While staying with Lem Barney; every day was a fresh learning experience. When we first arrived, Lem asked us if we had brought suits with us. Neither one of us owned a suit. Lem drove us straight to a mall and bought us both suits that first day. The next surprise was he didn't take us to a hotel. He took us into his own home. Lem's life became a part of my own life. I wasn't just left alone in a room somewhere waiting for celebrity photo opps. We spent quality time together. We shared meals, met and hung out with his son like I was part of the family. Lem introduced me to many of his own close personal friends. Yes, I got to see the fame side as well. I even got to attend the shooting of a commercial he was commissioned to be in. It was thrilling to ride along and participate in various celebrity functions and autograph signings with Lem as well.

But the real significance was not how much he showed me the glamour of celebrity life. No, it was how he used the time to really mentor me about what truly mattered. Living a life of influence. Even in the midst of his busy schedule he took time with me. He taught me a principle that has been a foundation for me in all I put my hand to even now. That we are all celebrities with degrees of influence. The defining difference is what you do with that influence for others. Lem told me that all celebrities are no different than anyone else. That I could have everything he did and even much more if I would apply myself to be a person of influence and never give up. And he constantly reminded me that no matter how successful I might become to always reach back to help someone else—always.

Those three weeks were a real pivot point that continues to testify about the bedrock of my success in life. Lem's lessons ignited a fire within me to do more. It will always hold a special place in my heart and soul.

I believe in giving honor where honor is due. Lem is an example that I aspire to be and I want to encourage other rising stars and people of influence to be like this too. Lem took me into his own life and home to let me experience personally one on one time with him. This put my life on an amazing trajectory to activate the same kind of transformation in countless other youth's lives.

People hear me say often that my organization is a place "Where every kid deserves a chance." I have lived that. Lem Barney made a decision to show a young kid from Southeast Raleigh that he deserved a chance to re-direct and re-focus himself for a life of influence. It birthed my vision to gather people of influence to intimately connect with youth to encourage, empower and mentor them to also become influencers in their futures,' families, careers, and communities. Influencing the life of a young person does not just stop at transforming their individual life; but every life they are destined to touch. This means that with enough influencers doing just that, we have the ability to change our communities and our world. This is what drives me in establishing a community legacy in every event, conference, field trip, and opportunity that Our Youth Matters creates for its youth today.

IT TAKES A COMMUNITY

Alfredo Hicks, *Childhood Friend, Raleigh, NC*

We grew up in the same area of Southeast Raleigh and we went to High School at the same time. Everybody in that area knew one another. And that's how I knew him coming up as a teenager.

I know him professionally through work and personally as the "funny guy" because Robert is the one to have a conversation with if you want to be in tears from laughter.

He is always hilarious and the life of the party. He's got a great, authentic personality and his humor seals the deal.

However, after attending one of his events I looked at him in a different light.

I realized he had another side other than just being humorous. That he is passionate about people and youth. He goes all in and does a staggering amount of work in the community beyond the job.

The community definitely needs more leaders like him. We need people that care about our community and care about the people in our community, especially the youth, because they are the ones who will be taking over for us at the end of our careers. We both are within a year of retirement, so to reach back and invest in those who are going to be taking our place is very important.

We have worked together now for over 25 years. And In our dealings we have come across juveniles that definitely could use some positive influence. Robert has taken that seriously. His passion for youth and the juveniles is something that he is sincere about and he doesn't brush anyone off. If he sees someone that he can help through his program that he sees is going astray—he will help them.

He is the father of two girls and I am the father of a son and a daughter and a couple of boys. What Robert has done and is doing makes you pay attention more to your own situation. To not only love the people outside of your home but that you gotta start at home. Seeing his efforts has led me to focus more on my personal life and being a role model to my son and now my grandson. Because many times I hear about people caring for kids outside of their home which is important but you have to clean up home before you can go outside. So, he has inspired my parenting. And that inspiration has helped me see the contribution I make to the community through my parenting and how I reach out to others myself.

The community landscape has changed so much leaving just the average kid in the neighborhood nowhere to really go freely. You know you could go to a center or a gym at any given time and everybody was welcomed in. Now things have kind of transitioned; everything is not just open to everyone in most communities. So these kids are left to figure out extracurricular things to do on their own because the opportunity to go to certain places is just not available. When we were coming up; if your Mom and Dad wanted to find you then they could just go to the community center or gym. But now if your Mom and Dad want to find you there's no telling if you're not at home where you are. Our parents they knew where to find us because our community center and gym were open to everybody and if you wanted something to do outside of sitting at home doing homework you could go to there.

Now we don't know where our youth are and there's no telling what they might be getting into. Somebody told me something that I think rings pretty true. People don't make mistakes; they make bad decisions. Youth today need someone who will invest in and teach them how to secure a better future through learning how to be good decision makers.

Robert is a very intentional innovator who has found the right mix of interesting and creative ways to congregate youth within environments that are positive, empowering and safe.

That is a need in our community now. We need more of that, and I am glad that someone with his dogged determination is at the helm of an organization like Our Youth Matters.

CHAPTER FOUR

YOU DON'T CHOOSE

"What extraordinary vehicles destiny selects to accomplish its design."
Henry A. Kissinger

The divine intersection of my life with Lem Barney's in 1991 literally catapulted my life into another orbit. After I got back to Raleigh from Michigan, my experiences with Lem Barney were not over yet. It was several weeks later when Lem called and asked if I could come get him at the airport. When he got in the car he asked me, "Do you know where Sheriff John H. Baker, Jr. lives?" I told him I knew where he lived but I didn't know him. When we got to the right house it was evening time. Lem jumped out of the car and started banging like crazy on the front door. Finally, Sheriff John H. Baker Jr. answered and Lem motioned for me to come on inside with them. We were sitting at the table together in the kitchen just talking when Lem put his arm around me and said, "John this is my friend Robert, I want you to watch out for him and be good to him." John replied, "I got him." It was because of Lem Barney that I met another celebrity that day.

John wasn't just the Sheriff but he had been Lem's teammate in the NFL as well. Here I was again sitting amongst people of influence, who were inviting me into their world. Lem flew back home and I went back to my house once again overwhelmed by the experience.

The next morning my Dad yelled for me, "Boochie! Telephone!" I picked up the line, announced myself and heard this: "Robert, this is Sheriff John H. Baker, Jr. I have a package down here at my office for you. I need you to come pick it up, fill it out and return it back to no one but me." I did exactly as he told me and went to pick up the package and returned it as he instructed me to. It was about two weeks later I got a call for an interview. When I arrived for the interview, I shook the secretary's hand and then sat down in a chair. I heard the Sheriff's phone ring and while he was on the phone he started laughing. After he hung up the phone, he looked over at me and said, "You're hired." It was 1992 when Sheriff John H. Baker, Jr. joined Lem's Barney efforts as another trail blazer who opened the door to a new direction for my life. My first 6 months was spent receiving office training, getting sworn in and doing my rifle qualifications, while I waited for the next entry season for the Academy. Once I officially entered the Sheriff's

Academy basketball jumped in the back seat. Now I was fueled with a passion for making my way forward in the arena of law enforcement. When you find your assignment in life, it attracts speed and builds tenacity in you.

At the Academy you have to take a state exam and you only get two chances. If you do not pass the second time you do not get paid and you lose your job. I spent days and hours upon hours trying to study for that exam. I remember how nervous I was. When I walked out the first time, I failed it. It was hard trying to encourage myself. My basketball dream had discouraged me. College had been ok, but it also did not deliver what I had in mind for myself. But then, I remembered I had a praying mom. She told me not to worry and to study.

So, my mom kept praying and I kept studying. Now when I took it the second time; the answers came to me like they had been marked on the inside of my mind. There was a confidence in me that I knew everything I needed to. After I turned in my exam paperwork and the lady in the office said I passed, I called my mom and could not stop shouting: I passed! I passed! I passed! She said, "Be quiet boy! I already know you passed." Then I called Sheriff John H. Baker, Jr. and told him I passed. He said, "Robert, welcome to the Sheriff's office!" It had been two years from the time I had my incredible experience with Lem Barney when I graduated from the Sheriff Academy in the Summer of 1993.

When I made the transition into the law enforcement world my Dad was happy. He told me, "You may not get rich but you will have a good job and you can keep a stable lifestyle and a roof over your head." My dad was extremely proud as was my mom. It still makes me chuckle when I think back on that. Most people might think that law enforcement was a natural choice for someone whose father had been a correctional officer. But that had not been the case since I only had eyes for basketball and the NBA. Remember I shared that my Dad had been a pretty rough and demanding kind of person, who spent most of his time at work. There had never been those types of discussions with my Dad that I got to have with Lem Barney and Sheriff John H. Baker, Jr. Their investment of time, face to face conversations, and idea exchanges had opened up a whole new perspective for me. I saw my career as a position of influence not just a job. I recognized my ability to choose the kind of person and officer I would become. My work would never rule me like a taskmaster the way it had my father. Instead I saw the possibilities of being empowered and empowering others.

I soaked up every opportunity to work in so many different areas of law enforcement. I learned the most about myself and my passion for youth when I worked as a bailiff. It was while working specifically in the juvenile court rooms that I began to develop an ear for the different cries of the juveniles. As I worked and trained through law enforcement for the next several years; a revelation began to develop. I started seeing how most of them, even though their behavior did not always give an obvious appearance of it, were attempting to reach out for help. I began recognizing how many of these youth were trapped in a system many of them did not understand.

Some kids did not know why they were locked up and they did not understand that they had committed a crime by doing some of the things they had been caught doing. I realized many juveniles only education about the criminal, probation and court procedures came from being processed through it. But there was not always comprehension of the details, language, and protocols. I am not in denial about how some can be. I can tell you that I have seen my share of youth and adults who are sick, need help, rehab, etc. But most of the juveniles I saw pass through the courtroom as a bailiff only had "getting into trouble" as their teacher and "repeat offender" as their mentor. What I started meditating on was this: what if some of these kids could be educated beforehand? What if they had the opportunity to experience and walk through the structures, rules, and methods of the law that they lived with in their communities. What if their life experience training could include: walk throughs of the Fire and Sheriff Departments, Clerk of Court Office, Social Services and Health Department or the District Attorney? If these youth could be taught to understand what the systems were designed for; then maybe the trauma, and life wrecking distress of having a record or rap sheet could be circumvented. There had to be a way to design innovative methods to educate youth so that fear and misinformed experiences were not their norm anymore.

I became convinced that I had to create something that modeled this kind of intervention to produce changed lives. Lem Barney and Sheriff John H. Baker, Jr. had mentored, educated and influenced me. They took the time to walk me through a completely different way of looking at my life and the journey I was on. And now I had been in law enforcement for almost 15 years. I had graduated from being empowered to the ranks of applying my learning and experience to empower others. These thoughts were the beginning of the next phase of my path in creating a legacy to help youth.

IT TAKES
A COMMUNITY

Clarence "Chucky" Brown Jr., *Former N.C. State basketball player, All-ACC first-teamer and NBA Champion,*

We call him Boochie.

I met Boochie when he was in high school, he played for a friend of mine- John H. Baker, III - Baker would open up the gym and we would all go over there and play and Boochie would be there, and even though he was a young kid he would play with us. That's how we got to know each other.

He might get mad that I am telling you this part but ya know I have to remember that he is grown now. However, I still call him Boochie now when I see him. I say, "Hey what's up Boochie?" I don't know how he got the name Boochie. It was the name he had when I got introduced to him. It's been Boochie ever since.

So whenever they would start talking about Robert Mitchener, I would be like who is that? And then I realized OH! You are talking about

Boochie. He will have to tell you that, make him tell you how he got the name Boochie.

What connected you with Our Youth Matters?

I knew Robert was working with the Sheriff's department. but he hit me up one day and asked me to be a part of an Our Youth Matters event. So, since I knew him and knew what type of person he was, I was ok with doing whatever he asked me to do.

I think it's a good thing that he is doing.

He always is so good at explaining what he has going and he's also passionate about it. Not only on the phone, but when you see him in person. You can see the passion he has about the youth. I know he has encountered many youth working with the Sheriff's department that have been going the wrong way and his desire is to make a positive impact on them. Because without our youth there is no future.

As a coach I understand his vantage point, you have to be a role model, you have to lead with something positive with these kids, because you never know what these kids might be dealing with. Some of the schools I have been at, kids come to school and they haven't eaten. Kids coming to you and asking if they can borrow two dollars because they haven't eaten. So, you give it to them and at the same time go a step further and ask the question, hey are you eating? Do you have what you need? Because maybe these kids don't have anything to eat at home, it might mean saying to that kid; "Hey let me take you somewhere and let's eat and I'll get you something." You never know what people are going through.

> *Money is great, but there's nothing more valuable than time.*

You hear people spending $500,000 a year and that's awesome, but what would mean more to people is if you came and gave them 30 minutes. Not 5 minutes, 5 doesn't say anything, but if you really want to make an impact come be with people who normally can't touch you or can't see you unless it's on a TV. Come spend 30 minutes with them, that will mean more and they will definitely never forget that. That's why I coach, That's exactly why I coach.

I am in this to share my knowledge of basketball and my knowledge of life, with other kids that are coming up so I can let them know you can do this if you put your mind to it. If you're not good enough to be a basketball player but you are good with sports there are a lot of other things you CAN do. You could be a sports agent, you could be referee, a timekeeper. You can do things that still keep you in the midst of the game, you could be a coach.

You know if I have a good kid that is close to making the team, I will make them a student coach, because he has dreams of wanting to be a part of the team, ok so I say to them you can put this on your resume later. That kind of opportunity has the potential of future building.

Many kids need to hear that we see something in them and that's why we are reaching out to say something to them, and if we didn't see anything we wouldn't reach out. Establishing that personal connection with youth helps them take it better when you talk to them, because it sets them up to accept input for their success.

Do you believe that Robert emulates that type of lifestyle leadership?

We were older than Boochie, so he saw how we were. When he got older, we were good examples for him. he has taken that and used it and effectively grown those examples into avenues of advancement for others. I remember how someone took the time to recognize what was in me and gave me an opportunity and it inspired me to take the chance (to become a coach). It has led me to do the same; to recognize what is in our youth and give them the opportunity to realize it.

Robert's strongest qualities with youth is being patient and listening to them...and he has a way of communicating with youth and building a rapport that gets them to understand better what they need to do.

Without a doubt I will back anything that is positive and what Robert is doing is positive. He has the makings of a true influencer because he is taking his lifestyle and investing it to help build the leader within others.

CHAPTER FIVE

THE CALL TO WHAT MATTERS

"Where your talents and the needs of the world cross — there lies your vocation."
Aristotle

By the early 2000's after wearing out most of my fellow friends, colleagues and co-workers discussing my research and ideas of doing more, I took a major step. I created my first program. I even had it copyrighted.

I had witnessed so many juveniles who through the courtroom or the streets were missing school due to being suspended or expelled. My idea was based on not removing youth from school but providing an alternative that would give them hope and help in furthering their education. I developed an experimental program that focused on developing goals and methods for actively engaging students in learning activities while they were suspended instead of having them sit and do nothing or worse telling them they had to stay home when many of them didn't have very good home lives. These kids needed mentors. Most people think of only what they call "the good kids" needing mentors. Have you ever looked up what the word mentor means? The Oxford dictionary says it literally means: "an experienced and trusted advisor or to train or advise someone, usually who is younger." Well, according to that definition anyone younger than yourself can be mentored. And if you have experience and the ability to be trusted you can be a mentor. There wasn't anything in our community that was giving this to these kids. Most communities won't consider working with the kids who have made mistakes. They prefer to let the system handle them. But I wanted these youth to see a different approach. The program also worked on providing services that could help build a bridge with whoever was at home, to assist the student and family as a whole. This program kept students accountable for working out their corrective actions but it also infused hope into their learning scenarios that went beyond just punitive measures. Youth will respond and rise to what is offered them when you plant the thought that they are still valued and can move in a positive direction, even though they have made a mistake or are in circumstances that may seem out of their own control.

I have always believed that it takes community to make change. So my program included the collaboration of families, the schools and the community. Youth could be referred by their home schools or by agencies that were working with at-risk students. We would work on providing them opportunities to re-direct their anger and disruptive behaviors through the power of learning better choices and achieving reachable goals. The program utilized after school hours and several weeks during the summer so that the endgame of reuniting these students back into their regular school settings could be realized. I called it the In-School Suspension Mentoring Program. My takeaway of the experience was this: the projects creation demanded budgets, money, line expenditures, policies, procedures and research criteria, admission requirements and launching proposals. And at the end of the day, finding people to come aboard with it was a challenge. You see, many people love to talk about how something should get done, but the crowds grow small when it's time for hands to begin the task. However, I had done my due diligence and would not let my idea just sit around until it was able to happen. I made the decision to expand it even bigger.

The next step I took was creating my own organization and non-profit to continue pursuing, finding, and innovating ways to fill the gaps I saw in reaching the communities young people. That is when Our Youth Matters was born. When my desire to commit myself to help, mentor, educate and develop opportunities for the youth I saw day after day and year after year was greater than all the voices that were telling me it just couldn't be done right now. I knew in my heart and believed that I could present a better way.

I designed a Community Support Day to introduce the In-School Suspension Mentoring Program to the surrounding areas. The unique twist was that it wasn't an event to only bring awareness about my own program but to expand the bigger picture and bring recognition of the numerous programs who were doing great youth work in the community but hadn't been recognized. I reached out to local High Schools, teachers, Judges, radio personalities, Councilmen, Businesspeople, Athletes, Coaches, organizations and people I had met and heard about who cared about working with youth. And I designed awards to give them to express gratitude for what they were doing and thanking them for continuing to do it. Ever play King of the Mountain growing up? The point is to be the only one standing on the top. My approach then and now continues to re-shape this kind of thinking. Collaboration is not about pushing people off the mountain so that the only thing seen is yourself. Too often in this world many only collaborate to achieve their own agenda. That will never build a community. There is great power in gathering those of like mind and labors together. When people, organizations and youth see that they are not the only ones it re-ignites them to go further.

It should always be about growing the mountain large enough for everyone to live and work together.

My mom, Barbara
Mitchener, High School
Graduation

Our Family: Valerie,
Cassandra, Jeanette, Me,
Mom and Dad.

Mom receiving an award. She worked at Memorex Telex and was
known for her inspiring work ethic on the job and in the community.

Dad, relaxing after a long day in his favorite chair.

Me and my Dad Robert Mitchener, Sr. in uniform together.
He was very proud of the fact that I became a law enforcement officer.

My Middle School Basketball Team photo. I am number 54.

Playing basketball has always been a passion. I loved being a part of a team. I still use those experiences to teach youth today.

#40-My favorite jersey
number to play in.

My elementary school
photo

Listening to my Coach during a High School game at Broughton.

My first grade school photo   I wore #54 on the CAPS
                                   Middle School Basketball
                                   Team.

My 4th grade class picture. Even back then I loved helping other kids.

*My High School
Graduation*

*I wore #40 for my
Broughton High School
Basketball Team.*

Needham B. Broughton High School Basketball Team. I am in front.

Chris Butler and I learning about music greats at Hittsville Motown.

It was a great honor to actually meet Mr. Kiyosaki in person. I have used many of his principles in my own life and to teach others.

Enjoying some Gala after dinner posing with friends in Detroit.

*Myself and good buddy Chris exploring Boston. I love travel and
I often encourage the youth I work with to do the same.*

At Lem Barney's house with his son, who made me feel at home.

Throwback from my security days, me and Don Jones backstage with Johnny Gill.

Attending a community focused luncheon with Joel Wiggins.

Charles and I at a Raleigh community event.

Attending a seminar with my longtime advocate councilman Eugene Weeks (l), Judge Ruth (r), and Judge Keith Gregory (far left).

Myself and Glenn Warren, CEO of Father Forever. It is an honor to serve the communities of Raleigh with dedicated men like Glenn.

Joel Wiggins (his wife is pictured right) is another Raleigh leader who shares my vision for better communities and families.

Attending the Community Hero awards banquet.

I had the honor and pleasure of meeting, the late Mr. York Sr. a well known real estate and community leader in the Raleigh area.

Myself and some fellow colleagues at a law enforcement seminar.

Getting to meet Kim Kiyosaki at an event in New England.

*It was an honor to meet and introduce the youth to the Legislative
Black Caucus at the OYM Summer Leadership Camp*

Law Enforcement Academy Graduation Day - 1992

Highway Patrol Driver's Training at the Law Enforcement Academy

Preparing for an Our Youth Matters Community Event.

A picture moment with some of the Our Youth Matters volunteers at the Youth Breakfast Symposium in Raleigh.

Signing Certificates of Completion for participants in Our Youth Matters

My Passion and Motto:

Changing Youth through Community.

Attorney Buch Williams and I at the Youth Symposium.

Youth Camp Field trip to learn about the Legislative Bill system.
They also participated in a Mock Trial proceeding.

IT TAKES
A COMMUNITY

Zell E. Lucas, *CEO of Lucas Transportation*

I am a retired engineer at ITT and I started my own business transporting children with special needs. So I met Robert talking to him one day about an experience I was having with one of my students who was about 15 or 17 years old and I said to Robert:

> *"Man I am dealing with this young man, and he is terrible; this young man is bad!" And Robert said:*

> *"Wait, wait, wait, hold it Mr. Lucas. He is not that, you can't say that, you need to get to know this young man. There is something in his past that is causing him to act the way he does."*

> *Even though Robert is a much younger man than I, I decided to listen to him right there and then. We had a conversation and Robert said:*

> *"You got to understand that this young man that you are dealing with you can't say that he is bad, just try to talk to this young man. Something is happening in his life that you just don't know about until you give him a chance to trust you and tell you."*

And that's how I met Robert Mitchener. He was a very outgoing person and always had a passion for young children, and getting them on the right track. It was a wonderful way to meet someone and I will never forget it.

So I went back and did talk with this young man and did what Robert said I should do. Then about 4-5 years after that I was at a convenience store on Newburn Avenue in Raleigh and someone with a heavy voice behind me said:

"Hey Mr. Lucas!"

So I looked around and it was that same kid that had grown up to be a young man, and he said to me:

"Mr. Lucas do you remember me?" And I said,

"Yes, I remember you." He said,

"Mr. Lucas you remember you told me I would probably end up in jail or in prison."

And I replied:

"Son, I am sorry I said that but you are right I did say that, 'cause you were giving me a hard time."

But then I asked him:

"Well, what's going on with you right now?" He replied:

"Well Mr. Lucas, I never did go to jail or go to prison, I have a job and I work for the city in Waste Management and I work on this truck and we pick up dumpsters on the streets and near houses and in residential areas. I am doing good; I have two children and I go to work every day."

This encounter happened I believe because I had taken the time that Robert advised me to take in talking to this young man. Saying something encouraging to him. I think I would have never had that conversation with that young man if it hadn't of been for Robert.

This is one thing I can say about Robert he always says don't ever give up on kids, you can't call them bad you just got to try to find a way to reach out to those kids. I think often about that time and about Robert and how he always lives out his motto of 'no such thing as bad kids.'

You know I am the older man who is supposed to give a man like Robert advice but I have learned to live and deal better with others because I chose to listen to him.

He is a very inspiring man and to be able to learn from someone younger than me has been a true gift and has motivated and influenced me in so many ways. I have taken what I have learned and what I am learning from Robert to share it with someone even younger than him, it's an awesome thing.

Whatever and whenever he is ready to do anything to reach out to kids, I've told him call me on the phone and I will be there. He is doing a good thing around here something we need more people like him to do. It makes me always willing to do something for him and with him to help Our Youth Matters. What he does has pushed me to get involved full tilt with this younger generation.

My experience with Robert even to this day in the work I do has continued to keep me inspired to always keep a positive perspective, attitude, and heart towards all young people—period. that I can't entertain thoughts that any kid is a hopeless case but that in all youth there is so much good to see that outweighs any and all bad that you might presently see. You can't look at any youth and label them bad because of the way they dress or because of how they talk, you have to see beyond these things and see the person that youth can become. Robert has really taught me this and it's a concept that has truly opened my eyes that I am grateful for.

No matter what someone is doing or has done, he always sees the best in anyone, especially young people. Robert doesn't treat children as though they should have an adult mind when they are only children, he sees that we have to encourage them where they are to spur the growth of their minds in the most positive way.

I have been among the youth in what many people call "the hood" who would gladly work and make efforts but we need those people who possess the substance of oppor-

tunities for them so that these youth have somewhere to grow the better side of themselves in an arena of hope, to feel valued and to experience the satisfaction of purpose. But that arena can only exist if people decide to do as Robert often says—to reach back.

I pray for Robert and his organization. Robert always mentions God in whatever he is doing that he couldn't do it without him. And I remember when Robert said to me he had only one year left at the Sheriff department and then he could do what he really wanted. To devote himself full time to these youth 100% when most people would take their retirement to do more self oriented things.

Remember every young person possesses a little piece of legacy within them. They just need someone to acknowledge it and help them connect it to the right place and purpose so the legacy within them has a chance to grow and not die off.

Robert has inspired me to simply DO SOMETHING. To not wait because the opportunity to do it may be lost if you do not ACT.

There's an old song by Harold Melvin and the Blue Notes, look it up some time; it's called: TIME TO WAKE UP EVERYBODY. The times sung about in that song really do compare still to our times even now. The call to help the children of the future hasn't changed so that must mean we are still the ones - YOU and ME - who have to change it.

Robert has been that for me...A wake up call to build and plant for a better future for our youth. A call to open our eyes to see them and help them while it is still called——TODAY.

CHAPTER SIX

HOW TO RESPOND TO LIFE

"The most characteristic mark of a great mind is to choose some one important object, and pursue it for life."
Anna Letitia Barbauld

When I first started Our Youth Matters, I began with simple events. I started with what I knew would be an immediate help and of interest to the youth and families of my surrounding community. Doing basketball camps, working with kids who needed a meal and place to be after school. Rallying volunteers, mentors and teachers to assist students who needed tutoring help with their homework and studies on the weekends.

Often the camps I created were welcomed because there are so many neighborhoods that do not have anything to offer youth. I also made sure to work out a transportation option so kids who had parents who worked or didn't have a car in their family could still have a means to get to the camp and participate. Learning your community and those kinds of basic needs are necessary to building relationships with youth and families so they can learn to trust your efforts.

So many youth and families today believe that no one truly cares about their situations or needs. I often would spend time walking around the camps during the activities checking in with the kids, volunteers and making sure that if there were parents or guardians or grandparents to connect with, then I did just that. It is not just about programs. It is always going to be about people. People may attend events and programs but how they experience your response to who they are and what matters to them is the glue of the relationships and legacy you are establishing with them. You never know how much of an impact your decision to respond to someone's need can make the difference and open a door for a young person. I say decision to respond for a reason. There are so many youth who are not learning how to bring the right response to the life they are living right now. Many youth today need us to respond to them not berate, judge, or speak at them, but to really connect on their level with an understanding that sees and cares about who they are.

I can remember one time when I was doing a summer camp for my youth program.

A young kid was dropped off by his mother, and we had breakfast that day, and no one had told me that he was the type who liked to run away. Not long after he finished eating breakfast, he left. The camp ended for the day around 4pm. As the volunteers and camp activities were wrapping up, his mother came to pick him up but the young man was nowhere to be found. After asking several of the kids and counselors; no one knew that he had slipped out or where he had gone. His mother simply said: "he does this all the time, and she left." I decided to go look for him. So, I rode around all over the neighborhood for what was close to an hour. When I got back to the camp area he suddenly showed up. I called his mother to come get him, telling her he was at the camp now. She could hardly believe it, but said she would be there shortly. As we waited together, I began to fuss him out a little bit. That's a southern saying for letting kids know about what they may have done wasn't the best choice. You know the drill, when you tell kids that people were worried and friends were concerned and it scares parents when they don't know where you are. But after all that, I said, "You think I don't want you back at this camp?" and he replied: "Yes sir, I got it, I know you don't want me here no more." And I said: "No, I want you back here first thing bright and early tomorrow morning because I love you and I care about you and I care about what happens to you." Then I gave him a hug. Do you know what happened next? He cried. Right there on my shoulder—and I let him. When he was finished, I hugged him again before he went home with his mother. Responding to youth with love and compassion in the midst of their mess and mistakes makes an unerasable mark. That kid ended up being the best camper I EVER had. He came on time. He participated and helped out with the other campers. If anything ever happened in that camp that I needed to know about, he would let me know. He was compelled to be better because I spoke to his heart not just his behavior. Youth know when you are speaking from the real place of the heart. That's the only place any of us really change is within our hearts. And that is why you must keep the heart of youth at the center of any work you engage in with them. Showing your heart towards them gives them something to believe in within themselves. Giving anyone this kind of belief about themselves changes their lives.

IT TAKES
A COMMUNITY

Tomiko Hicks *Wake County, HS-ESS Assistant Division Director - Child Support Services*

How did you meet?

I have actually known Boochie, I won't call him Boochie right now, but I have probably known Robert for like I can't tell you how long. My husband and I are Raleigh natives, and we were reared in the Southeast Raleigh Community, where Boochie was reared, and I can't think of a time where I did not know Robert Mitchener.

We are connected by community. My husband is in law enforcement as part of the Raleigh police Department. I actually work in Wade County as well. And so we are connected that way professionally. I work with Wade County Human Services downtown right across the street from the Sheriff's department. So we have a lot of ties that bind us.

We are friends who reach out to each other to talk personally and professionally. However we might need each other, he is actually one of my anchors.

In what ways do you work with his organization?

We share a common vision and passion for children. We have a common love of serving our community of youth. Making sure they get the love and guidance they need. We often bounce ideas off of one another of how to be a better resource to those in our community and what initiatives we both can drive home to reinforce each other in our endeavors.

In what ways has his organization inspired you?

Let's just say that I am extremely proud of the work that he is doing, I am in awe of the compassion he shows for the people that he is serving. Even though he has children of his own, he has extended his kindness, love, and care to the community at large. It takes someone with a really huge heart to provide care to others and to the youth of our community. Robert understands they are the substance of our future who will be responsible for leading the charge of caring for us in the future. Just seeing the work that he is putting in now to build a better community for us; I am very inspired by that.

How is Robert providing key opportunities for youth?

Just by his imprint in the community. Robert is constantly connecting the community with youth, and connecting the youth with people or areas that they desire to be in. And just being THERE - showing that he really cares about being involved with every aspect and phase of their life and showing them the things that they don't normally get a chance to see. He is always working on giving youth opportunities to meet with and connect with people they might not otherwise have the chance to encounter.

How important do you believe Our Youth Matter's and people like Robert Mitchener are?

If children are our future the failure to invest in children would mean a failure for our future. Robert is taking the investment that must be made in youth to new levels and pushing others to do the same.

I am so encouraged and inspired by it and I just think it's the most worthwhile thing you can do to help a child reach their goals and visions in life.

Though we don't get to see one another often; we each make a point to reach out to one another to keep up our connection. Maintaining connection is what keeps the pulse of community alive. We both recognize that. And because of our commitment to that, we can always pick up like no time has elapsed. If you ever need him, you can call and if he ever needs you he knows he can call. This is the type of relationship Robert desires to impart to our youth and community. Creating a community of close, personal, like- minded friends who cherish their connection to one another's now and future. I am so proud of him and thankful for him, and I am willing to help him shoulder the future of our youth and he knows he can count on me for anything.

CHAPTER SEVEN

CREATING MEANING

"Life is not meaningful…unless it is serving an end beyond itself; unless it is of value to someone else."
Abraham Joshua Heschel

My mother had gotten laid off from work. She had worked more than 30 years at Memorex/ Telex, a computer plant that made printed circuit boards. With being laid off she had no income. So, I opened up a beauty salon because I knew my mom liked to do hair and get her nails done and such. Once I got the salon started; I let her run it. She would collect the rent from the stylists and keep watch over the place. I remember a time when she needed help with bills, I asked her to do a fish fry. She thought we were going to split the money at the end of the day, but then I told her it was hers to keep. Helping my mom out like that taught me about how important purpose and meaning are to people. They are the currency to our souls.

These two important elements have become the bedrock of the events I have created over the years. When I wanted to find a way for kids to learn the legal system without being processed through it; that's how my Legislative Field Trip was born. I designed a tour for elementary school age children to participate in several activities within the judicial system. They got to take part in a mock trial where they each got to assume a role in a real courtroom. They were able to meet judges, bailiff's and officers in a setting that wasn't charged with fear or misinformation but a genuine understanding of legal protocol. Another aspect of the trip gave them the experience of seeing various speakers from different State departments and a live panel of legislators from the North Carolina Black Legislative Caucus. When youth are immersed into a setting they are charged with the energy to believe they can become what they are a part of. It's up to all of us to innovate and invent these experiences for them. Doing so exponentially effects their lives.

One of my biggest ventures in establishing and initiating this kind of result came from a Gala I created. Remember earlier in my story I shared with you about acknowledging others? Communities are living entities. When you begin to see your co-authoring partnership with those in your community that are already making a difference; you strengthen them, yourself and those youth and families that everyone is connected to. So, as I looked at my community, I began to really study it and then I found those people and organization's in the area whose vision and purpose were aligned with Our Youth Matters. But still it wasn't just about inviting them to hear about what I wanted to do or was doing. I made it about what THEY had been doing.

There are numerous heroes and heroines out there who deserve to be recognized for what they are accomplishing and for whom they accomplish it for. You see reciprocity is the glue and fuel of relational collaboration. Connecting with those who are like minded creates an atmosphere for innovation and transformation of the lives you all come into contact with. An example of this in action, is once I began to put together the layout for the Gala; the next step was creating meaning for those who would take part in it.

A Gala invokes images of luxury and honor. So, I started with hiring Ushers. No, I didn't go to a temp agency. I hired the youth I had been mentoring. Why? So they could have an opportunity to learn. Being an Usher is an experience in servant leadership. They were going to experience an event where everyone they were going to serve were also servant leaders in their community. At the Gala, these Ushers would get to see area Ministers receive awards for their Spiritual Leadership. Business owners, Athletes, Coaches and Teachers Community Leaders Awards. Even Judges, Artists and Corporate Executives receive Humanitarian Awards. And the most important element was that all of them were from the heart of the community these young men lived in.

Serving in the capacity of Usher, as I trained them, prepared them for making the connection that they could be one of these leaders too. I mentored them about etiquette, protocol, honor, and how to carry themselves among leaders. And I not only paid them for their time which showed them I honored their efforts to rise to the occasion, but I dressed them as well. Teaching them that certain leadership roles require being specially outfitted for the task. Their suits were all tailored to them, with special emblems as well just for the event.

I also founded regular Breakfast Symposiums where I gathered moderated panels of well known Community Leaders and people of Influence to speak to youth about topics like Service and Success in the 21st Century.

So, you see every event began to take on my passion of multi-faceted purpose. Raising awareness and funds, providing mentoring and acknowledgement. These experiences that Our Youth Matters initiated were creating an atmosphere where everyone attending, serving and being served, had the fulfillment of meaning and purpose. This is Community in action.

And my desire is for you to be inspired to study where you live and find the ways you can create meaning right in your own community as well.

IT TAKES
A COMMUNITY

Councilman Eugene Weeks, *retired, former member of the Raleigh City Council in North Carolina, representing District C. He served from 2010 to 2015.*

I met Robert as a student at Broughton High School in Raleigh. He was actually my student and I was his teacher. He was an outstanding student, I had Robert as my student for four years from freshman to graduation. He always showed leadership, he was very eager to learn and he tried to apply what he was learning in the class to his life.

I used to tell all of my students "Always remember you are a can do student."

Robert made the choice to take that to another level. Not only in the classroom but he was also a leader on the basketball team there. He was always an outstanding individual and he did not take anything for granted. He was a hard worker and he believed that he could achieve anything that he wanted to accomplish. That was a goal he continued doing not only at school but even when he graduated and decided to take on the challenge of creating his own programs.

Faith was definitely a part of what he was doing and I know that because he is a member of the church I go to as well. So from high school until now I have always been a mentor to him and told him he could always count on and call me whenever he needed to. There were times when he was going through trials and tribulations, as he was trying to set up Our Youth Matters. You know something? Robert built the organization not only with his passion but with his own two hands and money. He was so willing to go through whatever he had to help these kids achieve something like he did in school and in life outside of school.

Robert is so very committed to his passion, that it literally is all he desires to talk about, think about and dream big about. And he has never been just a talker but a doer of the things he speaks about.

And when the issue of the pandemic came about, and he was a bit down about some of the things that had to be cancelled, I told him don't worry, there will be years that you can do it. Go ahead and move forward with the things you need to do and can do now. Like keeping in contact with the youth and letting them know that you still care about them and that things will bounce back in the future.

What inspires me about Robert is that he is a go-getter. He will continue no matter how hard the task may be, he will continue to try to achieve what he wants to do in life and with this project Our Youth Matters. He is not one of those persons who will give up. Many people would give up the first time something went wrong, but he is not that type of individual. That's why I call him one of my best go-getters. he believes in that. I've seen it and its working right here in the city of Raleigh, I see it by what he's doing. And he still maintains his full time job as a Deputy Sheriff. He is representing the community in the workplace as well as representing the youth in Wade County and the city of Raleigh. That inspires me more than anything else; to see him striving to keep things going for the youth here in the city of Raleigh.

We don't just need more organizations like his we also are in need of more PEOPLE like him!

If we had more young people (I still call him young) to do what he is doing; more communities would become a better place to live.

Bottom Line Robert is a good listener, he will listen to you. I would often say to my students; "Are you listening or are you hearing?" He is a good listener. And even at his age he gives me the respect that one would give a father or member of his own family. That is another thing I genuinely like about him, and it is not only to me but he gives respect to any person he is communicating with. This is a rare thing to find in this day.

He also has worked tirelessly to keep connected and keep in contact with people so he could stay on point to plan and execute the programs he has planned. Many times I have helped him pray on it and to keep it going; reminding him everything will be ok. He has chosen to believe that and he continues to make actionable steps toward making events happen and they have—every time.

Robert is an individual above reproach. I am talking about his character, his integrity and his leadership. He continues to surprise and inspire me and every time I see him face to face I say to him, "You remembered what I told you in class!" He has never taken no for an answer and I've seen him accomplish his short range goals while still consistently working on his long range goal to be there for the youth. And he is doing that. Parents are seeing what he is doing and they are beginning to back him 100%. So not only does he have the students but now he is getting the parents involved too. They are seeing the urgency and results of pushing their sons and daughters to do what they need to do. Robert is truly inspiring parents to push their children to achieve their dreams. And not just the parents who are participating in his program but also the parents in the community who do not have any of their kids in the programs but he has begun a movement where he is helping others in the community to develop a better attitude toward creating a better landscape for the youth and their future. People are talking about him in the neighborhoods, churches, in the schools, he is a legacy builder and he is passionate about continuing to do it, building it up, and energizing others to do the same.

I could talk about Mitchener all day long, because when I see him bottom line, I see in him that I have achieved something in the classroom where I was teaching. As an educator that is inspiring to see something you have poured into become an establisher of better and greater things, and that's really the main thing.

The youth today are lacking mentorship, someone who can mentor and guide them along in different things in life, not as an interference to what parents are doing with them but when they step outside their doors, they need someone to mentor them about doing the right things so that people will not hear about them being locked up or falling into paths that lead to dead ends.

I would like to see that for as many youth that went through his program bringing services back to the city, the county and the state, I hope one day I will see some of these youth being sworn in on the city council, being sworn in on the county commission, and being involved with the various committees and organizations that are working to help and develop others within this region, if I can see that then I can say that this man Robert Mitchener has truly accomplished this thing he set out to do of establishing a legacy.

That people will not only recognize what he has done but begin to use his passion for legacy building as a blueprint for when they are talking about budgets, funding and things, that they realize they need to throw in money for developing youth programs in the city, the county and the state.

So these are things I am looking forward to seeing and for one day that Robert will be recognized (by the City, the council and

the state-though I know that doesn't matter to him) for what he has invested and accomplished on behalf of youth and others in developing a community legacy.

I have told Robert I am with him all the way with whatever he might need to announce, promote, fundraise, to help transport youth, make calls to people to get involved, and though I may not be able to be at the programs always, he can rely on the fact that I am backing him 100% on everything he is doing and will always be there for him.

CHAPTER EIGHT

LOVING YOUR PURPOSE: WIN, LOSE OR DRAW

*"The precepts of the law are these: to live honestly,
to injure no one, and to give everyone his due."*
Justinian I

One of my saddest moments was when my mother passed away. I still remember how it all happened. Remembering her final moments has given me a greater respect, appreciation and perspective of how her life influenced my own.

She was the one who made you get up in the mornings, and made you go to church. You *had* to be in church. In fact, the day my Mom passed away we were actually leaving church, and I was driving. She wanted to stop by the convenience store to get some Cheetos, a honeybun and a Pepsi cola.

I drove to our neighborhood store and went in to get her favorite snacks. It's funny how even to this day I don't know if she actually ate any of it. But once we got home, she started getting ready for her Eastern Star meeting that evening. She took my sisters car. The last thing I remember about seeing her alive was seeing her smiling as she drove out of the driveway.

When the house phone rang my sister answered the call and I knew exactly what it was even though I wasn't on the phone. I was laying across the couch and just trembling because I just knew what it was. My sister told all of us that my mom had collapsed and the ambulance was on the way. I drove my car to the meeting place. When we arrived, I jumped out of my car and ran all the way to the top of the stairs. When I looked inside the meeting room there was my mother lying on the floor.

I fell down on my knees beside her. All I could think of was all the times I had been able to help her; but this time I couldn't help her. I took her passing very hard because of that. I didn't eat and I couldn't sleep because every time I thought about her it would wake me up. I was like that for weeks. Finally, my good friend Alfredo Hicks came to see me. He told me I needed to snap out of it before I lost everything. It was one of the hardest things to make a comeback from. I remember thinking about how proud she was when I attempted anything; like school plays, trying out for Varsity, or the church choir. I thought long and hard about what she would think about me just sitting and letting everything go. She would not have wanted that. I made the decision to always hear her voice cheering me on the way she did all the years I had her. It's one of the voices I cherish and it still pushes me to strive to move further forward in whatever I put my hands to even now.

Getting divorced was definitely another one of the most difficult challenges that I went through in my life. It's very memorable not just because my marriage ended, but the way it happened.

It was my own daughter who walked out to my car and hand delivered my divorce papers to me, right while I was sitting in the driveway. She didn't know what it was that she had been asked to give to me. It was a hurtful day. We all need to keep watch over how we handle ourselves when children and youth are in our lives. Using children in adult situations that are beyond their ability to comprehend at certain ages, is detrimental to their own growth. It was a difficult road to talk through all of that. I wish it upon no one, adult or child. And the experience has kept me humble and ever thoughtful of what may be happening in the lives of the youth that I mentor and work with.

I had to find a certain tenacity when I lost my mother to move on with my life. I had to find that same tenacity to keep in relationship with my own children even when my marriage ended. Serving your community builds within you that same kind of tenacity. The kind of toughness that stabilizes you win, lose or draw.

When I started this youth program it was hard to get people involved. People often like to hear about your organization, its activities, and what it is you would like to do, but they don't always want to get behind you until they see it moving. So, when you decide to invest in your community, you must make the decision that it will cost you the investment of yourself on multiple levels.

In the early years; I would ask for donations, volunteers or help and many times it was a challenge. My first major event I decided to come up with the money out of my own pocket, because I had the vision and deep desire to see it come to fruition. And it did. I had a stage set up in the community at a local park and I invited the Southeast Raleigh High School band and several singers and performers. I had vendors, the fire department, the police department, and I even set up a booth for people to register to vote. It was a coming out event for Our Youth Matters where I was introducing to the community what Our Youth Matters was and what it wanted to accomplish for the communities young people.

Another event I planned and paid for out of my own pocket was for a summer youth camp. A local church wanted to do a summer camp for free for area kids. I gathered people and some were volunteers but some had to be paid. I used my own paychecks to get this accomplished even before I knew how I was going to get the kids fed for the duration of the camp. When extra funds didn't come in, I took the responsibility to pay for the food too. So, I provided breakfast and lunch each day and It would be a couple of weeks into the camp before I reached out to an old junior high school friend I had played basketball with and told him what I was doing all on my own. He agreed to pitch in with me for another couple of weeks to help make sure the kids got fed helping with breakfast and buying pizza's for the kids lunch. After that he helped advocate for getting the county involved to help the camp with food for the children for the remaining weeks of the camp.

I actually thought things were going quite well when someone gave me a building with power and said we could use it however we needed to. I gathered retired teachers and tutors to create a way for kids to have study help for homework, SAT's and schoolwork. And I even started providing food for that. Breakfast, donuts, snacks and lunch. Yet still I faced the challenges of maintaining volunteers and the setbacks of getting kids to participate or even show up. Many times I would get discouraged. Especially when time and again most of my events were paid for out of my own pocket, without grants, without any paycheck from the organization. But I had made a decision like I spoke about earlier; that my organization is my passion. I have chosen to be an investor in my community for the long haul. I never started all of this to get a paycheck; I started it for a purpose. And though grants and donations are welcome and good, I understood that my community needed my involvement *now* not only when others wanted to give or a grant decided to.

Additionally, I have never believed in charging any youth for anything Our Youth Matters has offered. I grew up in a family that couldn't spare money to do much of anything, extra dollars were for necessities and not much else. There are still many youth and families in that position even in our times today. We exist to help those who wouldn't otherwise have the opportunity. Our Youth Matters commits to keeping things free for youth as one of the ways

I have continued and kept my promise to Lem Barney, to always reach back and help someone else.

My stories I am sharing have one focus in mind. I am encouraging and reminding you of a very important principle in building legacy within your community. There are many people out there who are doing things out in the community, who are not getting recognized or receiving anything for what they do. People who are in the trenches everyday helping people right where they are in their own neighborhoods and many of them have not had their names in the newspapers, placed on any statues or plaques. Never forget that there are people out in your community who are giving out of their own supply to be a resource to others—win, lose or draw.

IT TAKES A COMMUNITY

Chris Thomas. *Legendary Comedian & Host of The Chris Thomas Show, Mayor of BET's Rap City*

How did you meet Robert?

I met Robert several years ago at an event I was performing at.

He came up and let me know how he enjoyed my show and began to tell me about how much he enjoyed working with and mentoring young people. And since I also have been to prisons and jails to talk to inmates and I've spoken with youth myself I was very encouraged by what he was sharing with me.

So many kids are basically raised without any direction or proper influence. They watch television, that's one influence, they walk into the street that's another influence, and when they come home, which should be their first influence...it's not, it's unfortunately their last influence.

Children are all God sent and born within them is a purpose that they are to do, and they learn to do it by following leadership

Robert is that rare kind of leader that is providing a model that youth can not only buy into but that they can and do follow-This is what matters.

So when Robert began to tell me about what he was planning to do with the school and helping young people, I told him an important factor is to get down to the WHY of what these kids today are going through.

It's all about programming - what programs a child. Television, movies, social media these unfortunately have become a part of the daily onslaught of what is programming kids about how life is supposed to go. And the question is: Are their parents or guardians stepping in to say what is real and what is not? Too often youth are not being directed in a manner that encourages their life. So, the work is in figuring out a way to get them unprogrammed from the fabricated fictions they are currently consuming to a life programmed by truth, directed by purposeful goals and fulfilled dreams. Robert is a living and breathing example of someone who is dedicated to re-programming kids to live out their best truth in spite of their circumstances.

My goal is to help Robert develop what he is doing so it can be replicated in numerous other communities so they can do it the way he is because what he is doing and how he is operating is a successful model.

Why not keep the recreation center open all night and then have a room or two where you can give classes to kids or people who may be interested in a bunch of things, but they haven't homed in on what it is.

You have to help get kids off the streets yes, because some of them are living lives where they do commit crimes just to eat food or have somewhere to lay at night or through the winter, I knew a guy who led the life of a criminal because by doing it he got fed and had some place to lay his head. So that is what became his programming.

Something else I am trying to help Robert do is get to the bottom of what is going on with young people and adults today because it's not only the ones who don't have anything that are dealing with wrong programming, we have rappers, athletes, artists, etc. all who have millions of dollars and their minds still aren't right because of faulty programming in their own lives too. So they can shoot a basketball, or throw a football, or whatever and everything else about how to live life in excellence has not been a part of their programming or been a factor in how they should conduct their own lives.

How do we help kids; especially when most of society wants to shut down?

We have to begin giving kids an understanding of not only what is good and bad, but we need to begin to give kids direction so they can move on from being passively programmed by their circumstances and actively engaged in programming themselves with better thoughts that help them produce better actions and in turn begin the important work of new beginnings for a new generation of youth that are empowered by the encouragement of their ideas instead of enslaved to their current situations or surroundings.

What do you admire about him and what is he doing that makes a difference?

Some people have that old saying that you can only help a few, but Robert is one of those people who truly believes that ALL can be helped... This is the kind of belief system so many of us need to begin to follow ourselves, that no one is beyond being helped and no one has to be left behind anymore. He is a man who knows by experience through seeing so many youth go through things that don't have or should not have to happen and instead of allowing his heart to be jaded or calloused by it, he has chosen a higher road to rise above being hardened to what he has seen and instead he has turned it into a passion for seeing change materialize.

How do you feel about Robert, Our Youth Matters and its future endeavors?

How many people in law enforcement are still wanting to work with kids (young adults, men and women) after seeing them on the wrong side of things? Robert has seen thousands of these kids going through all facets of the incarceration process and he is trying to help them. He is making the effort to see that there is another side to the story by digging his heels into the community to find out and make changes from the base place right where they are and live. How many are doing this? This is why I wanted to become a part of what Robert is doing because I desire to see this develop and help my own community establish it where I live.

Too many are being born into situations where there is no plan and that only gives them two choices - incarceration or death - Robert is trying to stop that cycle and start a new pattern where these kids can experience a life and a future, how could anyone not want to be a part of that? Resurrecting a new beginning in the life of a young child or teenager...*that's* legacy building at its best. Helping kids find the best self of who they are and giving them a purpose to strive for. Too often today people are too absorbed in themselves. It's time for a new direction.

This is why I am so glad to be a part of helping him and that passion come to fruition the best way I can. I have chosen to utilize all the connections I have and the people I know to help his effort and his movement of Our Youth Matters to continue to move forward in giving today's youth a purpose that causes them to breed purpose and fulfillment in their future homes, families and communities.

CHAPTER NINE

CHANCE, CHANGE, AND INFLUENCE

"Great things are done by a series of small things brought together."
Vincent Van Gogh

My goal has always been about turning a chance into a change. So many kids are out there shooting baskets in life thinking that change isn't possible because life only has a limited number of chances. I want to be the type of person who helps people see the chance in their hands as an opportunity to break away from their life situation statistics. To show kids that with the right moves and choices they can stack up chances in their favor.

What are some things you think you might do if you had the chance? And how many times would you try again if you thought you had missed any number of chances you had failed at making or failed to take advantage of? I want to open young people's eyes to consider that their chances haven't run out and change is always possible no matter what the situation.

Tell me, does your neighbor know you? Your neighbors kids? Anyone who lives just a stone's throw away from you. How well do they know you? Do they think you care? What if you had a relationship with them? What would be different about their life? About your life? What would your connection produce? A cup of sugar, flour or an egg borrowed. A civil acquaintance for pleasantries at the mailbox or garbage can? Are you or have you ever considered becoming a trusted friend for their time of need or even a catalyst for the next step in their destiny? Have you considered being more than just a contact number in a list or a calendar reminder for a non-social task line up? What would happen if you placed more value on your neighbor, than just the real estate you call home?

You can probably check off many accomplishments you have racked up on the job: CEU's, workshops, webinars , etc. But what has any of that added to anyone else's life in your sphere of influence? What would you be capable of creating if you stopped for a moment to build lives and not just build a winning brand version of yourself? What if you could brand a legacy of changed lives in your performance profile? If each of your 401k dollars were a person, what would they be saying about you once you began to withdraw them from their account? What tangible interest have you built up in people that dollars can never buy or pay for?

How do you really get to know someone? You share your hopes and dreams with one another. Too many of us think that you can only share those things with people who are close to you, and there is something to that. But I'd like to challenge you about who you consider is close. Many youth today need a close place where they can be listened to and heard, and if you can open your eyes to see those "close" to you, you just might discover the next big idea or next iconic inventor, or influencer right next door to you. Try talking with the youth around you and "close" to you about some of your own dreams and plans and how they did or even didn't bring you to where you are now and strike up the fires of imagination in another person. That kind of action starts a chain reaction that builds communication, then community and then legacy.

Just like Lem Barney my mentor did for me. I was a youth who had a Dad that wasn't mentoring me because he didn't really have the time. There are many youth in this exact same scenario. But Lem Barney took the time, and in those few weeks with him he changed my life forever for the better.

A mentor is focused on building a relationship and leading others into becoming the best version of themselves. Youth need to know that their existence matters in this world. They need direction and guidance to do this. Celebrities and people of influence need to consider how they themselves can grow if they direct their efforts to the work of growing others beyond an event or a featured promotional gathering.

Connecting on a tangible long term level that contributes real life changes in the lives and hearts of others. Imagine that your time spent with them is an opportunity to deliver them out of what they are in and into their dreams and purposes. What value can be placed on helping a young person believe that all of their hard work and determination is going to help them make it and make a difference.

No kid would ever forget if a celebrity or person of influence would do that for them. They would begin to think that if someone like this is willing to come into my atmosphere and tell me I have purpose and value then I can do anything. This is something that celebrities and people of influence can begin to plant into these kids hearts and minds. The belief that their current realities can change into better ones. This kind of investment can blow a kid away and ignite them to work harder at being focused on achieving their goals and dreams.

I do realize that many celebrities/people of influence (social, economic, political, and athletic) do give and donate so much money, which is great. Sure, the money is good. But Time...TIME. Have you ever noticed when a kid who is growing up with a parent(s) who work all the time, and their basic needs are met? But if you ask that kid what they want most, they always say the same thing. They want to spend TIME with their parent(s). They are not thinking about the money or things; they are always focused on TIME.

I am entreating celebrities and people of influence everywhere to consider looking more closely at how they can interact with kids beyond just their brands and the things they sell and promote.

Why? Because these kids as they are growing up eventually are going to come up short on the return of their investment. The exchange isn't the same measure or quality of return. Their dollars are enriching the lives of others but how is what they receive as an exchange (shoes, clothing, bling, swag, etc.) translating to a return of the investment into their real time lives that really matters? What about their investment propels them to the next level of developing as a person beyond material things and promotional perspectives? This chapter has asked you the reader a lot of questions. This was intentional.

I want this chapter to leave you with your mind running. I am challenging you to look around the neighborhood you call home. Begin considering all the chances you can create. The changes you could initiate. And most importantly, I want you to begin making influential actions toward legacy to build innovative connections within your own communities to Make Youth Matter.

IT TAKES
A COMMUNITY

Mrs. Doris Frazier, *Retired Educator/Tutor, Raleigh, NC*

How did you meet?

I was Robert's Middle School English teacher. He was a fine student, I don't remember all my students because I taught for over 30 years, so I don't remember them all, and even after I stopped teaching, I did afterschool tutoring for students. And now I have been retired 20 years, but Robert certainly stands out in my memory. It was because he was always very dedicated to his studies, helping other students, and he was always pushing them to do better without being pushy if you know what I mean.

He could always get on their level and talk them into doing the right thing and wouldn't let them get in trouble. It makes me smile when I think back on one of his friends from Middle School who had gotten in trouble as an adult. You know what? Robert has from what I have heard tried to help him too. He was then and he still is always helping someone. And Robert has always been a gentleman, even when being involved with people he wasn't a tell them what you should do type of person. He was always leading them by example in the right direction. And those were times I remember from his Middle School days. Later on, I saw him again through his High School days because I was involved with the High School he went to. And always when we spoke; I would tell him how proud I was of him doing so well in school.

He was always just a fine person, a very fine person. Another memorable moment that I had with him was when I had a special program at the Middle School where we brought in speakers from different careers. He came representing as a community law enforcement officer and brought along several other students from our school who are now in law enforcement as well. They spoke to the kids and it was quite meaningful for us to see how well these former students who had come from the same areas many of the kids listening to them had come from. I was so moved as a teacher about what they had accomplished but also, I think it had a great impact on those students to see the possibilities of what they can do and how our alumni students had done so well.

Now, I see him from time to time just in passing and I've always been really thrilled when I see him on television doing things with the community. I always say that's my Robert! So yes, he's been a fine young man from the time I'd known him in Middle School and I am just so glad that he is helping other student's because he certainly was a role model for people and students back then, so I know as an adult I can have great confidence in his ability to provide a great service to the community and its youth.

I am happy for Robert, and his wonderful organization that he has. I was delighted to hear that he was doing a book and certainly want it to go far. And I have always told him to let me know what else there is, so I can make a contribution and whatever else there is I can help with that I can do. I am very impressed and very proud of him for the young man he was in middle school and the man he has grown up to be doing meaningful things for students. I am definitely proud as an educator to see a student I poured into, now take the time to reach back and develop our young people coming up behind him and his generation. I give him my best!

CHAPTER TEN

LEGACY THROUGH COMMUNITY

"You can design and create, and build the most wonderful place in the world. But it takes people to make the dream a reality.
Walt Disney

When I created the In-School Suspension Mentoring Program, I always had in the back of my mind that it would eventually be something so much bigger. Though its initial run was short-lived, my vision to expand it has never ceased and only increased.

I am convinced that God does not bring any child into this world to become people who live lives of perpetual crime and punishment.

They are brought here to this world with dreams and goals. And for those that have lost their way, there must be those who answer the need so many youth have right now for re- direction back into their destined purpose.

I began thinking about what I could develop to get these kids to turn around. What could I invent or start to help solve the issues I was seeing every day, and year after year over the span of my own life-long career in law enforcement?

That is when my dream got big...REALLY BIG. I made the decision to figure out how Our Youth Matters could create its own school.

After many years of working in the multiple systems already at work in education; I realized it would need to be a private charter school. This would ensure that the school could belong to and benefit the community. This type of empowerment would then fuel local families and people of influence to be involved in the education of the young people right where they live.

I envision the school having K-12 grades and also a grade 13. This would allow for youth who need that extra mile in sharpening their skills for their next steps either into college or a vocational skill.

I believe that God has placed me in the earth to create opportunities. Developing this school for youth would help them to discover their gifts, talents and abilities. Establishing an education model that supports their dreams and goals to flourish.

You have read about some of the experiences Our Youth Matters created to help educate youth about their world. Beyond the normal amenities of gymnasiums and auditoriums and classrooms, this school would include modeling experiences such as: an on campus courtroom for youth to learn the legal, political, and legislative aspects of society, for the school clinic to have ample facilities to give early trainings to future therapists, medical students, nurses, and practitioners, science labs that connect youth with engineering and scientific mentorships, and a vocational center for integrating local artisans and apprenticeships, or conference rooms where youth can learn about contracts, corporate business and entrepreneurship. These unique aspects would generate for the youth a greater learning horizon and present a broader lens of choices for their futures.

The schools focus would also center on forging relationships that surround youth with better influences and caring mentors to connect with so they are encouraged to reach their goals and stay focused on achieving their dreams and a better life.

A lot of our youth today focus on the TV or their phones. They look at every kind of media and it is all filled with stars of every variety, and so many famous people that they look up to.

But now it's time for those who have that kind of power to inspire on another level. The ground level. I am not saying that no one does anything. We all are aware of the many celebrities and people of influence who are doing great things. However, I am asking everyone, not just those who are famous for their influence, to consider how they can spend real quality time with the youth of today in more meaningful ways. I would like those relational partnerships Our Youth Matters forms to follow the example of what you have now read about Lem Barney doing for me.

What if you spent several weeks out of your year to partner with a school of this kind as a mentor. So many colleges have fellows and scholars who have mentors. What if we created that kind of learning at the youth level? The changes to the landscape of our society's young people would be phenomenal with that kind of *involvement*.

The work of creating legacy is this: To first be involved yourself, and then to encourage local and global communities to get personally involved with building their future. This means everyone engaging together in tangibly felt actions to raise up a better standard for young people. And through these active community relationships; youth can receive the empowerment to transform themselves into dynamic leaders who shine as a beacon for those coming after them.

Many people have tried to tell me over the years that you can't save them all. Yet, working in the community and making an effort in the lives of these young people every day is a far better task to work diligently on; than continuing the contribution of our legacy of youth to the streets, jails, or cemeteries. I have seen too much of the latter over the three decades I have spent in law enforcement.

I believe that now it is my duty to put out a call to all those who are everyday people, celebrities, athletes, politicians, entrepreneurs, ministers and the many local and global people of influence to consider building a legacy together. Establishing communities that intentionally grow new cycles and paths of learning to launch youth into achieving the greatness they were born for.

"Every young person deserves a chance to fulfill their dreams; because when dreams are realized legacies are born."
-Robert Mitchener

IT TAKES A COMMUNITY

Courtney Crowder, *Managing Director, Apco Worldwide. Raleigh*

He is Boochie you have to ask him where that came from, I really don't know. I really don't remember ever not knowing him. he was the older cousin of a friend of mine and we all grew up in Southeast Raleigh. he stood out and was unique in the neighborhood since he was involved in law enforcement and because he was always nice. A big, nice, engaging person with a smile on his face who always left an impression even as a kid.

How does his organization inspire you?

He is the guy who is never too busy to give back. He recognizes that investing in kids by talking with them early and helping them see beyond their circumstances, is critical to their individual success, and ultimately the success of families and communities even.

He always manages to find a way to create opportunities and space for other people.

The vision and goal of his organization is plainly stated. It puts the purpose of the organization front and center. Knowing him, his values, his commitments, is what definitely made me want to be a part.

What are his values?

Community, Young people, Mentorship, He values not only telling people to do the right thing but helping make the connection to do so. He is definitely the type of person who puts his money where his mouth is, he lays it all down to approach things and he is both unique and appreciated.

Are organization's like his important to the community?

They are essential to the community in order for it to be healthy.

Promoting ways for communities to uplift themselves and their families, by teaching them how to wrap their arms around young people literally and figuratively - IF you are going to say you are about people then your either going to go above and beyond what he is doing or jump in and support what he is doing...

What pushes you to get involved the way you do? Because I know and lived it. I have been there.

There's an element of lifting while climbing that presents a better way of promoting positive things in the community, and you know and recognize that personally, financially, education and resource wise you have benefited from a lot of shoulders that you got to stand on. So becoming and taking my place among the lineage of those that want to be a set of shoulders for youth to come on board and stand on is the reason why I get involved.

If you could sum up Mitchener in three words what would they be?

You mean Boochie...lol Three words I would say:

Sincerity, Commitment, Community

What is the most important thing youth can gain from this book he is writing?

They should learn how to care for people, learn how to be selfless, and how to bless somebody because you've been blessed. Being an example of selfless commitment motivated by love for others.

Any other comments?

If you could combine a trailblazer award and a public service award and wrap it up in a lifetime achievement award. How do you give someone an award who would gladly take that award, turn around, and give it to someone else in need or who needed it? What can you give a person like that? The only things you can give to a person like that is your time, treasure and talent.

> *He is color blind, ability blind, blind to all things except that there is good in everybody. He is a truthful example of selfless commitment motivated by love for others. HE is a good man and a good person...it's actually true...that is what he is in every sense of the word.*

What would you say to help rouse those in the community to use their shoulders to help Robert and what he is doing?

I would get up and read like 45 three word sentences (subject, verb, and predicate) all the way down the page; with all the excuses, caveats and explanations. Then I would finally ask; Now, what are you going to do? It's not even that hard, you know?

It's not just about rousing people. It's about encouraging people to do what they know to do. Do what they know needs to be done. and then you don't have to explain it. You won't have to put it in context or wait for the next election cycle. You start doing what needs to be done because it needs to be done. You don't have to ask permission or apologize—That's it.

I think a lot of times folks get caught up in explanation; but at the end of the day what you say isn't truly the thing that is motivating you if you have to explain it. But if you are just doing it then it's simply self-explanatory. What actions are you taking every day?

People in their communities know exactly what is at stake, so what are you going to do about it? It's not totally complicated when placed on the right effort level.

EPILOGUE

Talent: Becoming what you Discover

"Legacy is not leaving something for people,
it is leaving something in people."
Peter Strople

Earlier, I spoke about the big time basketball player who I thought all my prayers and dreams were skipping over me to them. They lost everything and though opportunities arose, things still have not *yet* gotten back on track. But I keep telling them that for the young kids, there is a story that can be told. Remember the police officer who pulled me over? Later on, during my years serving as a court bailiff, that same officer approached me and apologized for what had happened. It's another moment in my life I won't **ever** forget, and I know my father would have been glad because of how he stood up for me. We all have stories in us that can benefit youth.

I think God gives everybody talents, and sometimes he gives those talents early on in life. Some take the talent and don't know how to steward it. They underestimate the determination, discipline and dedication required to manage their talent. And then others take the challenge and do something major with their talent by investing, nurturing and growing it into influence.

When I was growing up, I thought I needed the talents of those I saw and watched on TV to turn things around for myself. Then I came to the understanding that my talent was the passion to help and serve others. And now I know I don't have to become like anyone to use it.

God gives us talents to help people. Your talent is not for you to keep to yourself until you come to the end of your time here and leave this earth and the talent just goes with you when you get buried--NO. The talent is supposed to challenge you to target those around you every day in a way that is positive, purpose filled and inspirational. Passing on your talent to others, especially youth, is a part of the legacy building mandate on all of our lives.

So, discover your talents. Then invest in them, nurture them and grow them into influence and innovative ideas to build legacies for the youth in the community where you are. And if you live here in the Raleigh area, we hope you join the many dedicated volunteers and influencers among us in **Making Youth Matter.**

ABOUT THE AUTHOR

ROBERT MITCHENER

Mr. Mitchener has extensive training and education in all aspects of criminal justice and law enforcement to include screening, triage and referral to corrections and prison systems, specifically targeting at-risk adults and youth. He has 12 years of providing supervision and oversight development for community-wide law enforcement programs, solving law enforcement system issues and ensuring policy.

Consistent with law enforcement outcome models and new initiatives. He has a vast knowledge of criminal justice and gang violence prevention.

Mr. Mitchener graduated from Needham B. Broughton High School in Raleigh, North Carolina. There he was an exceptional athlete who lettered in basketball. He was accepted into Allen University in Columbia, South Carolina where he studied Business Administration for a short time until after his encounter with Lem Barney decided that law enforcement was his calling instead.

Mr. Mitchener's training includes: Law Enforcement Training, VIP Security, Investigative Procedures/ Techniques, Outstanding Team Management Skills, Presentation/Report Preparation, Critical Problem Resolutions and State/Federal Regulation Knowledge.

Robert proves his commitment to youth through his active efforts of creating, designing, hosting and funding events, camps leadership initiatives and mentoring in the community. Robert knows that children with mentors are more confident and have fewer behavioral problems. Robert is very passionate in his goal to help youth recognize and comprehend their self-worth to position themselves for a better future.

COMMUNITY SPONSOR TESTIMONIALS

State Level

"...I am excited to hear of your agency's interest an efforts regarding the creation of additional opportunities for court involved adolescents to enhance their interpersonal skills and talents through exposure to citizens who can (potentially) serve as mentors for success. On behalf of our local office, as we have referred many youth to your agency for participation in activities and programs, I convey to you our support as a community stakeholder regarding your ongoing efforts to invest in our State's greatest resource...its children..."

Donald W. Pinchback, *Chief Court Counselor, ACJJ District 10, North Carolina Dept. of Public Safety*

Corporate Level

"We will support and provide small meeting facilities for after school meetings and programs associated with Our Youth Matters. It is our hope that we can work with students leveraging our expertise in hospitality to enhance their etiquette skills, giving them a taste and vision of travel...We look forward to working with you and Our Youth Matters. We believe in your values and mission."

Leon Cox, *General Manager, Sheraton Raleigh*

"As a father, attorney, bank director and community leader in Raleigh, I have seen firsthand the need for youth to have strong mentorship, guidance and positive activities to put them on a firm foundation and the right track...Our Youth Matters provides just that. I am proud to serve as a community sponsor for Our Youth Matters..."

Charles T. Francis, *Attorney, The Francis Law Firm, PLLC, Raleigh, North Carolina*

Community Level

"...I am so glad you came over to our table at D&S Cafeteria. I wanted to express how you sounded so hopeful and positive. Also, I like the fact that you enjoy working with children. That's great because our children need someone who is really interested in their well-being and their future...I just wanted to write to tell you to be encouraged..."

Barbara Richardson, *Community Resident, Raleigh, North Carolina*

"...It gives us great pleasure to endorse your program along with its initiatives consisting of working cohesively with the National Youth Chamber of Commerce in efforts to educate each child and prepare them to continue their education and sustain a wholesome relationship within the household. The Brothers of Mentor Lodge #55 would be delighted in assisting you and your efforts making sure that each child succeeds and becomes a champion inside and outside of the classroom..."

Richard Limehouse, *Worshipful Master, Brothers of Mentor Lodge #55, Raleigh, North Carolina*

Business Level

"Our children have a mentor on whom they can rely…and the youth reacts positively to him and his ideas. "Our Youth Matters" gives the kids a chance to work on projects which will benefit them and our community. I transport thousands of students every year and I have seen how one man; one organization can make the difference in our children's lives. "Our Youth Matters" is that organization. The activities, the leadership and fellowship is outstanding."

Zell Lucas, *President & Founder, Lucas Transportation, Inc,*
Knightdale, North Carolina

"…I appreciate the service and selfless work your organization provides in the community with our youth…I am willing to partner with Our Youth Matters in offering community support services in life skill development and college preparedness. There is a need for youth awareness and the services your organization provides. We are here to support your mission…"

Yalanda P. Moore, *CEO, Healing Interventions, Inc.*
Raleigh, North Carolina

I WANTED THIS BOOK TO ACCOMPLISH THE FOLLOWING:

To show how God's plan can intersect your own and lead you toward the mission and destiny that He wants for you to affect others.

For every reader to know that even with all the places I've gone to and the people I've met; this has all been a God adventure. Nothing but God has placed my feet every step of the way and He continues to bless me every day.

When you choose the right perspective then you can accept and embrace the choices God sets in front of you.

To always everyday be the same person. On good days and on bad days. Choose to be your best self 100% all day every day.

Showing appreciation, respect and honor for different people, no matter the situation, ensures that you will reap benefits for doing so later on in your own journey.

That you have experienced being encouraged about your own ideas to help today's youth.

That you are inspired to act on some of the ideas and opportunities you have read about in this book in your own community.

Where Every Kid Deserves a Chance

The Mission of Our Youth Matters is to provide academic support, cultural enrichment and leadership development opportunities for students and families. We welcome new prospects and innovations to encourage and empower young people. Please reach out to us with your ideas or questions you have about becoming involved.

Our Youth Matters is a 501©3 organization. Gifts and donations are greatly appreciated and tax-deductible. We also truly value those who desire to give of their personal time to our youth and their success. Contact us directly to speak with us about your donation(s) of time, treasure, service or talent.

Call: 919.795.8609

Write: rmitchener70@gmail.com

Visit: www.ouryouthmatters.org

Friend/Follow: @OurYouthMattersusa
Support: rmitchener1@hotmail.com (PayPal)

$RobertMitchh (Cash App)

Notes

Notes

Notes

_____

_____

_____

_____

_____

_____

_____

_____

_____

Notes

Notes

Notes

Notes

Notes

Notes

Notes

_____

_____

_____

_____

_____

_____

_____

_____

_____

_____

Notes

Notes

_____

_____

_____

_____

_____

_____

_____

_____

_____

_____